W9-BMY-986

Dorothy Day

# Dorothy Day

## Writings from *Commonweal*

Patrick Jordan

*Editor*

**THE LITURGICAL PRESS**
Collegeville, Minnesota

www.litpress.org

Cover design by David Manahan, O.S.B. Photo of Dorothy Day courtesy of Marquette University Special Collections and Archives, Milwaukee, Wisconsin.

Pages 352–5 from *The Long Loneliness* by Dorothy Day, copyright 1952 by Harper & Row, Publishers, Inc. Copyright renewed © 1980 by Tamar Teresa Hennessy. Reprinted by permission of HarperCollins Publishers Inc.

© 2002 by *Commonweal*, New York, New York. All rights reserved. No part of this work may be reproduced in any form or by any means, electronic or mechanical, including photocopying, recording, taping, or any retrieval system, without the written permission of *Commonweal*, 475 Riverside Dr., Room 405, New York, NY 10115. Printed in the United States of America.

1    2    3    4    5    6    7    8

**Library of Congress Cataloging-in-Publication Data**

Day, Dorothy, 1897–1980.
    [Selections. 2002]
    Dorothy Day : writings from Commonweal / Patrick Jordan, editor.
      p. cm.
    Includes bibliographical references and index.
    ISBN 0-8146-2875-3 (alk. paper)
      1. Day, Dorothy, 1897–1980.   I. Jordan, Patrick.   II. Commonweal.
III. Title.

BX4668.D3 A3 2002
267'.182'092—dc21

2002069480

*For Tamar Hennessy and her family,*
*and in memory of*
*Edward S. Skillin and Thomas J. Sullivan*

# Contents

*Peter Maurin always says that it is the duty of the journalist to make history as well as record it.*

Dorothy Day
*Commonweal*, November 3, 1939

# Introduction

WHEN DOROTHY DAY DIED on November 29, 1980, at the age of eighty-three, historian David J. O'Brien described her as "the most significant, interesting, and influential person in the history of American Catholicism." It was a bold evaluation for a historian so close to the events and to the death of the person in question. Yet it remains perhaps the most perceptive, succinct, and often-quoted summation of Day's long and eventful life.

That O'Brien's appraisal appeared in the pages of *Commonweal* was fitting. Considered one of North America's premier Catholic publications since its founding in 1924, the independent lay Catholic journal of opinion played a pivotal role not only in the history of twentieth-century American Catholicism but in Day's personal and professional lives. *Commonweal* printed a broad range of her work over a span of nearly half a century (from the time of her conversion in the late 1920s through the mid-1970s). More significant, it was *Commonweal*'s managing editor, George N. Shuster, who first introduced Day to French-born social philosopher Peter Maurin (1877–1949) in late 1932. The following year, Day and Maurin launched the Catholic Worker movement, one of the most inventive and enduring lay experiments in American Catholicism.

The radical (that is, "back to the roots") Catholic Worker movement tapped into the core of the Christian gospel with a remarkable zest, applying the spirit of the New Testament to the social issues of the time, as well as to the quotidian concerns of family, work, prayer, and community. The movement and its monthly paper, *The Catholic Worker*, which Day edited, inspired scores of like-minded groups and publications in the United States and abroad. At Catholic Worker houses, the hungry were fed and the lost were welcomed. And so it continues today. Maurin and Day presented a profound critique of post-Christian society's materialism and militarism, and offered an alternative, not only in the movement's various publications and urban houses of hospitality, but at its rural communes and retreat centers. The effects are still being felt.

*Commonweal* ("the common good") had been inaugurated just a decade earlier as a weekly review of politics, religion, and culture. Modeled on the *New Republic* and the *Nation*, *Commonweal* signaled a novel undertaking in American Catholic publishing. It exemplified a new confidence among American Catholics, particularly the laity, that they could sustain a high-quality journal of opinion, independent of hierarchical control yet faithful to Catholic tradition. Embracing the American principles of freedom of inquiry and expression, *The Commonweal* (as it was known until 1965) became a forum for exploring controversial issues in a respectful, even ecumenical, manner that, then as now, was marked by its civility, vigorous thinking, and engaged writing.

When Day began her freelance career with *Commonweal* in 1929, she was already a seasoned journalist and editor. She had served on the staff of a number of leftist journals and was a published novelist. During and immediately following World War I, she had been a member of the Greenwich Village literary scene and a sometime political activist, having been arrested with both the suffragists and the Industrial Workers of the World. In 1926—following a broken love affair, an abortion, a rebound marriage that ended in divorce, and a common-law union— Day gave birth to a daughter, Tamar Teresa. Later that year, Day had her baby baptized a Catholic, and the following year she entered the Church herself. These decisions severed Day from Tamar's father, from her radical friends, and from professional associates, many of whom questioned Catholicism's dogmatic beliefs and its historic alliances with repressive regimes. By the time Day's writing began appearing in *Commonweal*, she had worked as a student nurse, a part-time cook, a Hollywood screenwriter, and had moved to Mexico with her young daughter.

Despite her personal upheavals, Day's early *Commonweal* articles demonstrate her journalistic self-assurance and her gift for narrative. Her eye for detail and social setting were matched by an astute sense of self-understanding. Day's first *Commonweal* pieces, written several years before her introduction to Maurin—whom she later called her teacher in matters of the spirit and of Catholicism—nonetheless reflect a personal and spiritual depth that foreshadowed her mature views and style, including a vivid love of Scripture and familiarity with the lives of the saints. During her later Catholic Worker period, Day fused these qualities with passionate criticisms of the state, racism, social inequity, and war, all of which subjects she addresses in this volume.

Reviewing Day's 1939 book *House of Hospitality* for *Commonweal*, Chicago priest Reynold Hillenbrand noted that four things emerged from reading Day: "the author's love of the poor; her struggle to get on with herself; her dedicated response to the beauties around her; [and] the unforgettable picture of [Manhattan's] Lower East Side." Hillenbrand concluded that Day's volume was not only a practical commentary on social doctrine, but that it was good spiritual reading. The present volume has the same strengths.

Day's language was seldom pietistic. On the contrary, her words could be provocative and intentionally unsettling. In reviewing her 1952 autobiography *The Long Loneliness* for *Commonweal*, H. A. Reinhold observed that Day loved "the inflamed and the inflaming word." Although Reinhold did not make note of it, Day could also be mistaken. In *The Long Loneliness* (a selection of which appears here; see "The Story of Steve Hergenhan," page 121), Day noted that in 1932 she had covered a demonstration of the unemployed in Washington, D.C., for *Commonweal*, and that at the same time she had reported on a convention of struggling farmers for *America* magazine. In actuality, she reported on the farmers for *Commonweal* (see, "Real Revolutionists," page 39), while writing about the unemployed for the Jesuit weekly.

For decades, Dorothy Day was part of a formidable roster of *Commonweal* authors that included the likes of G. K. Chesterton, Willa Cather, Lewis Mumford, Jacques and Raissa Maritain, Evelyn Waugh, Virgil Michel, O.S.B., Georges Bernanos, Walter Lippmann, Hannah Arendt, Graham Greene, Helene Iswolsky, John Cogley, François Mauriac, Anne Fremantle, W. H. Auden, Thomas Merton, Michael Harrington, John Updike, Walker Percy, Philip and Daniel Berrigan, and J. F. Powers—to mention but a few. Other than *The Catholic Worker* itself, no other journal published as many of Day's compositions (thirty-eight) over such an extended period (forty-four years) as did *Commonweal*.

The articles reprinted here—some for the first time since their original publication—serve as a short but nonetheless representative compendium of Day's interests and insights. They range from the personal—those dealing with her young daughter will open a new dimension to some readers—to the polemical; from youthful enthusiasms to the gratitude of an aged warrior. Included are brief book reviews, a short story, sketches from works in progress, letters (some of them withering) to *Commonweal*'s editors, portraits of prisoners and dissidents, and a gifted reporter's dispatches from the flash points of mid-twentieth-century social and economic conflict. To all these Day brought her characteristic ruggedness, an eye for the human particularity, and an intense thirst for the Absolute.

This collection also provides a sense of Day's impatience with systemic injustice and with political cant, while revealing her qualities of personal delight and vulnerability. She was never one attracted simply to intellectual constructs or rhetorical formulations. Rather, she was a reporter of daily realities for whom faith, hope, and love were tested in the roiling crises of her Catholic Worker experiences, her travels, and her witness—all beneath the shadows cast by the grimmest of centuries. To issues both immediate and great, Day brought a sense of full attention. In so doing, she changed lives and made history.

At its best, Dorothy Day's writing is bracing, evocative, and instructive. This anthology offers an overview of her perspective and attractiveness. It underscores O'Brien's assessment of her charm, magnitude, and prophetic contribution.

Patrick Jordan
Managing Editor
*Commonweal*

# The Brother and the Rooster 1

IT WAS HARD for old Brother Stanislaus to get used to new ways, the new rule, of the religious house in America to which he had been transferred. Every morning he arose at five and went to the chapel for half an hour's meditation. After Mass there were fifteen minutes for thanksgiving and half an hour for spiritual reading. Then before breakfast he had time to milk one of the cows. After breakfast there were fifteen minutes in which to say the Joyful Mysteries, then there were the other cows to milk and put out in the fields, and work in the vegetable and flower gardens until twelve, when there was another half-hour for spiritual reading before dinner. It was good to sit in peace and calm and cool off a bit, and very often Brother Stanislaus napped soundly instead of reading, which was but a venial sin, since it was without due deliberation and full consent of the will.

After dinner there were the Sorrowful Mysteries to be recited, followed by three-quarters of an hour of recreation. The long afternoon was spent in the garden or fields, or in the winter at carpentering or house cleaning. There was always plenty to do.

Supper was at six-thirty and the Glorious Mysteries completed the rosary for the day. Recreation followed, but Brother Stanislaus always used his time to water the garden. There was never enough rain. Evening prayers were at nine and the bell for retiring was rung at nine-thirty.

Originally published in *Commonweal,* September 18, 1929. Vol. X, 501–3.

The Polish brother soon learned to speak English as well as he spoke French or Italian, though never as well as he did his own language.

There were twenty-five novices, five lay brothers and three fathers in the House of Our Lady of the Sea. When the work was heavier than usual the fathers and novices joined in, making hay, cutting lawns and weeding the garden. For the first five years Brother Stanislaus was in America, he worked with the animals and vegetables. There were five cows, two horses, some ducks and chickens. It was hard for him to make friends with the other lay brothers who were much younger than he. But one dear friend Brother Stanislaus had among his charges and that was a young rooster, which he had raised and petted until it grew to know him and used to come and perch on his shoulder when he called. Every morning when he went to open the door of the chicken coop, it ran out to him, crowing in a friendly manner, strutting before him and showing off its fine feathers.

"God has given us a very fine morning," Brother Stanislaus would say to his little brother, the rooster. "Now if He will only send us a good shower this afternoon so that I won't have to water the garden tonight, I'll be very happy. My arms ache from carrying those heavy watering cans."

And the rooster crowed lustily as though to say, "Let us praise God at any rate. Whatever He does is very good."

At the end of five years Brother Stanislaus was transferred to the kitchen to work as cook with the help of another brother to do dishes and set the tables. This was a time of hardship for him. He had no great love for food, and he did love the out-of-doors and his animals. There was barely time in the morning to go out and greet his rooster before he had to start breakfast. The huge pot of oatmeal had to boil for an hour and there had to be tea, coffee and chocolate. There was time for Mass and spiritual reading during the meal, but there seemed to be no time for the half-hour of meditation.

Since he believed with Saint Teresa that the devil would shun any-one who was given to this devotion, it upset him to think he had to miss his morning exercise. It was impossible for him to get up earlier than the rising hour of five. He was an old man and very tired at the end of the day. So he had to take to meditation while he waited for the breakfast to cook.

"Good Saint Joseph, don't let my oatmeal burn," he would murmur, every now and then as he paced up and down the kitchen meditating on the Visitation, or the Four Last Things. And Saint Joseph watched over the stove and by seven the oatmeal was done to a turn and not sticking, at that—so that the pan was not hard to wash.

During the long winter it was not so hard to work in the kitchen. The big range heated up the room and it was pleasant to come into the kitchen in the morning from the icy bedrooms and the cold chapel. The singing of the tea kettle, the bubbling of the boiling potatoes and the noisy crackling of the roast in the oven were pleasant accompaniments to the peeling of vegetables and the cleaning off of closet shelves.

The worst thing about the kitchen work was that it was never finished. There was food to be prepared and cooked and the pots and pans to wash, and the kitchen to sweep and mop and the shelves and drawers to clean out and the windows to wash and the fire to keep up. Every minute of Brother Stanislaus's day was taken up. In the winter it was easier because the kitchen was a comfortable place—and because canned goods were used, which made it unnecessary to clean and prepare so many vegetables.

But summer was a time of penance. The long hot days made the stove a torture rather than a comfort. The kitchen was like a furnace with its three windows facing east and no direct draught through. The fresh vegetables to prepare for thirty-five people made the work seem interminable, and when the work of preparing vegetables and fruits for immediate consumption was done, there was the work of canning them.

Life was hard but Brother Stanislaus endured it all cheerfully, smiling at the thought that by his present sufferings he was expiating his sins here on earth instead of in purgatory. He was glad to suffer, happy in his discomfort. And when the orchestra of cicadas made the air ring with their hot tunings, he took his vegetables out on the back porch or sat on the grass under the trees in order that he might the better hear them at their work of praising God. He was happy even in the sound of the buzzing flies. Their hot drone reminded him of Italy.

There was always time, too, for visits with his little brother the rooster. Sometimes a moment before breakfast, another visit to throw the chickens their vegetable peelings. After supper, during recreation time, Brother Stanislaus sat on an old stump under a tree smoking his pipe and conversing with his friend.

He was alone in the world, very much alone on his pilgrimage. Once in a while he thought of an early boyhood friend of his in the religious house in France. They delighted in holy conversation, and used to vie with each other in making up spiritual bouquets to give to each other and to offer up to God. They loaned each other books—they read nothing but devotional works—which took them months to read and ponder and converse about. They delighted when the work was hard, and when there was not enough work, they spent long hours on their knees, even when their souls were dry and it seemed as though only meaningless words came from their hearts. When it was a struggle to pray, they delighted in prayer the more, because it was an added hardship overcome for the love of God.

But now Brother Stanislaus was all alone in this world and very sad. It seemed to him a mournful thing to be unhappy in a world which was often so beautiful, but he accepted his unhappiness and lack of consolation with resignation.

"'Life is but a night spent in a wretched inn,'" he said with Saint Teresa.

When he was very lonely he tried to dwell on thoughts of heaven and the companionship of the saints he would have there. When he cooked he cooked with loving care, as though for Saint Francis of Assisi and Saint Clare, Saint Anthony and Brother Juniper. He liked to offer his food to the Holy Family, giving Mary a respite from her humble work, and when he had made a nice supper, he used to say, "There, Saint Teresa, it's a wretched inn, I'll agree with you—but here's a nice supper for you to sit down to after your journeyings."

But though he believed and practiced in the communion of saints, he did not realize that his little rooster had more reality for him. His rooster became his companion, his treasure and his toy. When it came and perched on his knee, he talked to it as a little girl talks to her pet doll, he handled it lovingly as a bibliophile handles a precious volume; he exulted in the markings and shading of the bird.

Brother Gerard was a younger man than Brother Stanislaus, and had taken his place in the care of the cows, the chickens and the garden. He was a hard-working boy, but often absent-minded and careless, and when one morning Brother Stanislaus heard one of the fathers tell him to kill some roosters for Sunday dinner, he resolved to be present in the barnyard and help Brother Gerard catch the roosters.

"Be careful of my little friend out there," he called to the other brother as he was scalding out the milk cans in the pantry. "Be sure and let me know when you want to catch them and I'll come and help you."

But Brother Stanislaus spoke such broken English that it was hard for others to understand him, and since Brother Gerard was busily engaged while he worked in saying some extra prayers for a special intention, he scarcely listened.

"He is too holy," Brother Stanislaus muttered to himself over the dish pan. "He is as bad as Brother Juniper."

During the course of the morning he ran out often to the barnyard which was quite far away from the house, but always Brother Gerard was somewhere else, so that he could not see him to remind him again.

By noon, Brother Stanislaus had scorched the beans, burnt the roast and worked himself into a state of grievous irritation against life and Brother Gerard.

It was always hot and messy work, killing chickens, and Brother Gerard wanted to get it done before dinner so that he would not have that task to look forward to during the rest of the day. So while Brother Stanislaus was confined to the kitchen during the last critical half-hour before dinner, the other brother caught his chickens and killed them, saying fifty Hail Marys while he did so, to make the nauseous work easier.

Brother Stanislaus could eat nothing in his fear and uncertainty, and since the rule of silence was observed during meals he could not re-assure himself.

Immediately after, ignoring the bell for prayers in the chapel, he made his way to the barnyard. His heavy cassock which he put on just before he left the kitchen, over the denim kitchen apron in his hurry, twined about his legs and impeded his hurried step. He stumbled up the little hill, and slipped on the newly cut grass which cluttered the narrow path, so that he fell to his knees. His heart was constricted and he panted as he hurried along.

When he reached the yard and called, his little brother the rooster did not answer him. He could not have escaped so Brother Stanislaus knew the worst.

Sitting down heavily on the stump of the old tree, he felt the world suddenly very empty about him. Song sparrows were singing in the trees overhead and in the fields the meadow lark trilled her piercingly sweet tune. The cicadas, the bees, the buzzing flies, even the stirring of the leaves sounded unfeelingly gay and hostile to Brother Stanislaus. The sunlight was brazen and the wind jeered among the laughing leaves. His hands trembled as he took out his old pipe, and his heart was bitter and angry within him. His little pet, his tender joyous little rooster, who alone out of all the world had a loving heart for him, was gone. Brother Stanislaus wept.

He sat there for a long time, while the numb feeling turned to anger and the anger turned to remorse. He sat there still longer to say some prayers for the brother whom he had been hating so fiercely. He said them unfeelingly, because he knew he ought to say them, and he prayed for a heart of flesh to take the place of the stone in his breast.

"It is God's will," he kept murmuring, and finally he knew indeed that it was God's will, and was able to get up and go back to his pots and pans in the kitchen.

Two days later as he put his little friend in the pot on the stove for a fricassee, he said to him, "You are all I had, and I am offering you as a present to God. God alone knows what a lonely old man I am."

And that day, in some mysterious fashion, God made himself felt to the old lay brother, and his heart, as he wrestled with pots and pans, was full of joy.

# Guadalupe

2

"TODAY," I ANNOUNCED to four-year-old Teresa, "we will go out to see Our Lady of Guadalupe."

"A pil'mage?" Teresa asked hopefully. Pilgrimages to her whether in New York, California or Mexico, mean very delightful bus rides, and in general a spirit of festivity. "I will bring Mary flowers." She always speaks of our Blessed Mother in a most familiar way. And forthwith, she began to strip heliotrope blooms from the plant which blooms in my French doorway, looking out over the roofs of Mexico City.

I put a stop to this depredation, telling her that we would buy flowers from a little boy in the market, but she stubbornly clung to a few, too short-stemmed blossoms.

Teresa is at a very precious age, the age when the apocryphal stories tell us that Saint Ann introduced the Blessed Virgin to the temple. The little girl Mary danced up the steps, the story says, and I remember it often when Teresa is inclined to be full of antics in church.

Busses are always crowded, but more exciting than street cars. We got in at the Zocalo, in front of the cathedral, and within a few blocks, two sheep got in too, or rather were pushed in, for their feet were tied together, and they lay on the floor of the bus at our feet, surveying us patiently. In front of the driver's seat hung a picture of Saint Christopher, and beneath the picture a little vase suspended for flowers. We were reassured by the presence of the Saint, for the bus careened madly

Originally published in *Commonweal*, February 26, 1930. Vol. XI, 477–8.

around corners, past other busses, narrowly escaping pedestrians, urged on by the shouts of the conductor at every corner, "Vamonos," and by a vigorous slap of his hand on the tin sides of the camion.

The conductor is a gentleman beneath his rags. He gets out of the bus to help old ladies on. He lifts off the babies and children. He holds the market baskets for the women going home from their shopping. At one time, he had three gayly bedecked baskets, full of flowers, tomatoes, squash, one with a rabbit and still another with a live chicken, and in spite of his armful, he managed to collect the fares and help people on and off.

Teresa's enthusiasm was infectious. She squealed loudly at the spectacle of the lambs, the chicken and the rabbit. She wanted to know why there wasn't a pig.

"I'll sing a little song—all about a little pig riding on a burro, and all the little pigs have dirty faces—and that is Mexico."

No one could understand her song but the passengers laughed with her and the man next to us said, "Muy contento," and asked us where we were going.

Though the busses race along at a delirious speed, they are not impolitely hasty. If the driver sees anyone a block away indicating by gestures that he would like to come aboard, he stops to wait, and takes out a little top, which spins in the air, a "jo-jo" it is called, and which all the men and children are playing with at this time in Mexico City. But not the women. They have no time to play. They go to market and to Mass. They are always washing clothes. When they have nothing else to do, they are fanning the charcoal fires in order that the men and the children may eat.

Guadalupe is only a few miles from the center of the city, not as far as the Bronx is from lower Broadway. It takes only twenty minutes to get there. Though Christmas and Epiphany are passed, it is always a holiday at this shrine of the patroness of Mexico. December 12 is Guadalupe Day but the pilgrimages are not confined to the holiday season. Throughout the year tens of thousands of devout natives with their padres, come from distant cities in special trains to worship at their Virgin's shrine. As our Lady of Lourdes revealed herself to the poor peasant girl, so did our Lady again reveal herself to the poor peasant Juan Diego, filling his tilma with roses that he might convince the bishop—it was so long ago that it was the first bishop of Mexico—that his story of her appearance was indeed true. When he dropped the roses out at the feet of the bishop, his tilma was imprinted with a glorious picture of the Virgin, which is just as bright and glowing to this day as all the bright prints and reproductions which hang in every home, in every shop and market and place of business.

In front of the cathedral where the picture is enshrined are many booths where rosaries, candles and pictures are sold. On one side is a huge covered market which spills out into the streets for blocks around. On the other side there is a park where a Ferris wheel and merry-go-round accompany with their clamorous music the prayers of the faithful in the church. And in the back, there is the hill of Tepeyac where the Aztecs lived before the Spanish conquest. Now the hill is surmounted by a cemetery and on the top is a lovely little chapel which looks out over the entire city of Mexico, surrounded by the mountains, of which the greatest are the Mujer Blanca and Popocatapetl, crowned with dazzling snow. Nestling close to this small church are many little adobe houses, built on the side of the hill.

After Teresa had blessed herself with holy water, and made her rather lopsided genuflection, she skipped out of the church again that she might lean over the low walls and peer into doorways at the chickens, pigs, lambs and pigeons, not to speak of cats and dogs which shared the houses and gardens.

"These are all Mary's babies," she said. "The little pigs and the chickens and the boys and the girls. And these are all little baby houses, and that," pointing to the church, "is the mama house."

It had been a hard climb up the slippery cobbled steps of the little hill, and we were glad to sit there for a while on one of the terraces looking down on the pueblo of Guadalupe. On a pilgrimage the devout Mexicans will climb that hill on their knees, but on ordinary days like this they content themselves with a lesser penance. When they enter the cathedral at the foot of the hill, they advance on their knees all the length of the church to the altar, holding aloft a lighted candle in their hands. Many mothers have bundles on their backs as well as babies in their arms as they humbly pay their respects to the Mother of God.

When we descended the steps on the other side of the hill, there was still the holy spring to visit which is sheltered by a chapel domed with glazed tile. The spring boils up in the bottom of the walled-in well, and Teresa leaned over it fascinated. Attendants brought up water in copper buckets and poured out jugs full for the Mexicans and Indians who surround it at all times of the day, in order that they may drink.

"And oh, the tiniest baby church!" Teresa shouted, looking across the street where the littlest and humblest of chapels has been erected in honor of Juan Diego. There is room for only eight or ten people in it and it is the width of its doors which always stand open. Teresa had to say one of her tiny prayers here, "about you and me," she explained, and then she was ready for the bus again.

"And now, no more churches today," she sighed, surfeited as even the great saint for whom she was named confessed her weak flesh at times to be—"but a lollypop and peanuts instead."

# A Letter from Mexico City  3

O UTSIDE THE SUN IS POURING down on the roofs so that our several fat kittens seek the shade of the calla-lilies, heliotrope and other potted plants. I sit half in the shade, half out, just within the door which opens on our balcony and looks out over all the roofs. It is cold in our old stone building, and too hot outside. Soledad, the twelve-year-old girl of the house, is washing sheets in the flat stone laundry tub in the entry way, singing very cheerfully a gay Spanish hymn while she works.

Around her neck she wears a funny little rosary, as so many of the children do here—fifty tiny wooden beads, marked like cork, and a lead medal imprinted with a church like a wigwam, and two fir trees on either side. You buy these only at Guadalupe Villa, in front of the cathedral, and the prayers you say are directed of course to Our Lady of Guadalupe.

On every balcony there are cages of birds which do not sing, but whistle shrilly and call like parrots. Boys carry a dozen of them at a time on branches and they make no attempt to fly away. It is said that they are loaded down with small shot so that they cannot fly, but Señor Gomez, Soledad's uncle, says that they do not mind. It does not hurt them, but rather helps their digestion. If they did not have shot to eat, he says, they would eat gravel and small stones. They are very fat and healthy looking.

Originally published in *Commonweal*, April 16, 1930. Vol. XI, 683–4.

Last week, on Candlemas day, there were many cages of them hanging in the church. When the bells ceased ringing at the Elevation (and the clamor is as loud as two small boys can make it) you could hear the birds too, calling out piercingly, greeting the advent on the altar of their Maker.

Every morning I first go to the old church of San José, and thence to the market, just as all the women do here. The Nino Perdido street cars pass the church, so named not for any lost child of the neighborhood as I thought rather tragically at first, but for the lost Child Jesus, when He was separated from His holy mother and foster-father for three days. Nearby there is also the street of the Little Fishes, recalling one of the miracles of Jesus.

If one goes to eight o'clock Mass there are as many men as women in the congregation. But at the nine o'clock Mass which I usually attend, there are only a few men, mostly those who work about the streets and whose occupations give them more liberty. But the church is always thronged with women and children. There are those whom I presume to be sisters of some order, by the way they take charge of the children, and by the way the children kiss their hands as they take leave of them. You cannot tell them by the devout expression on their faces, because so many women of Mexico are marked by a quiet serenity.

Every day groups of women assist at Mass with scapulars six inches square about their shoulders which they take out of their market baskets when they enter the church and put back again when they leave. Another thing one notices—almost all the women assist at Mass with missals. They say the rosary in the church every evening, and not at Mass as so many in the United States do.

There are elegantly clad women, always in black, and many so poor that they must go barefoot on the cold stones of the church floor. Several barefooted little girls come in, and they have only one shawl between them so that they put it over their two or three heads and kneel together all through the service.

There is no formality during the service. The littlest children sit and play, silently of course, on the steps of the altar of San Antonio or Our Lady of Soledad. Many kneel at the altar rail all during the Mass, to be as close to the Blessed Sacrament as possible, and they do not interfere with those who wish to communicate, for the priest stands in one place at the foot of the altar, at the altar rail, and gives the Sacrament to the faithful who come two by two. At some special feast, indeed several times a week, the women bear lighted candles in their hands, which they extinguish after Communion and put back in their market baskets.

Communion is given before Mass, during Mass, and after Mass, and then the Sacrament is placed in the little chapel of the Sacred Heart where all day there are always scores of people worshiping with lighted candles in their hands, their arms outstretched. Many of the devout proceed on their knees to the altar rail.

It is strange to see the priests on the streets in gray or brown suits, and different colored felt hats, a grim reminder of those desolate years of persecution. The marks of that time are on all their faces. There are no young priests here.

I went to see Father Twaites, an Englishman who has been here for thirty years and who is now an old man, and when I reached his house I had a hard time gaining admittance. The porter professed to misunderstand me, and it was only after questioning several people that one woman whispered fearfully, "El Padre?" and showed me where to go. The people still tremble for the liberty and lives of their pastors.

There was a marriage in the church last Wednesday. A woman of the people with a black shawl over her head, knelt by the side of a tall cartero and after the marriage service the altar boys placed a wide satin scarf over her head and over the shoulders of her husband, and over that a white satin rope, knotting the two of them together for the rest of the Mass. An old barefooted Indian sat at the organ, with three little children kneeling beside him, and played and sang Gregorian plain chant—by ear, for there was no music in front of him. After Mass, several men with stringed instruments played hymns in which all the congregation joined and the music was happy and triumphant.

Though there is no discussion among the people as to what is going to happen or as to what has happened between Church and state—the attitude, as I have said, is still fearful—there is much talk against the administration.

Señor Gomez, the very intelligent business man who is the uncle of little Soledad, says that the people are not at all satisfied with Ortiz Rubio. "They may talk about the election being a democratic one, yet 75 percent of the people do not want Ortiz Rubio."

We hear this many times from people of all classes.

"The reason he went to the United States, everyone says, was to escape assassination," Señor Gomez went on. "He himself fears it. Didn't he say as he was leaving the palace, just before the attempted assassination on the day he was inaugurated, 'They can shoot at me now, but nevertheless I am president'? Many people think he will not last very long. They feel that Calles has put him where he is, and they do not wish to be imposed upon. Shall I call us a reactionary people? I mean that we react against imposition. Calles wanted his hacienda—he wanted to remain in the country instead of leaving it as so many ex-presidents have had to do. So he put a man of his own in his place. He is safe now, he thinks. But he and Ortiz Rubio are far from safe."

On the other hand Vasconcelos seems to be popular with the people. He is a man of vivid personality, they say, and wide interests. To me he is an enigmatic personality. What I do not understand is why he commissioned Diego Rivera, the artist, to decorate all the public buildings when Diego is an avowed Communist and a bitter anticlerical. However, Diego has painted many noble pictures of the religious who have helped to uplift Mexico, among the frescoes in the Secretaria de Education, in addition to the savage ones directed against the clergy, whom Rivera holds are hand in glove with the capitalists to keep down the people.

There is great accent placed on the friendly relations between Mexico and the United States. The city is full of tourists and many entertainments are planned in their honor. There seem always to be delegations of business men and newspapermen in the city; in many cases, their expenses paid by the Mexican government. Just this morning I stopped in one of the many bureaus of information and came away with a half-dozen gorgeously illustrated books and calendars about Mexico, written in English for Americans and distributed free.

One pamphlet consists of a very beautiful calendar, "civico," to distinguish it from the religious calendars the people have in their homes. On every other page there is a picture in black and white by some prominent and popular artist, including many of Rivera's. One picture is of Sor Juana Iniz de la Cruz, by Tamiji Kitagawa, calling the religious, *"sin disputa, el mas importante de nuestras letras coloniales."* Another by the same artist is of Fra Bartolome de las Casas. There is still another of the nativity by Clemente Orosco. It is significant that two of these religious pictures are by Japanese artists, and the one by a Mexican artist, a picture for children, of the toys of the nativity which are sold in the Alameda. There are no religious holidays marked on the calendar, though Epiphany was a public holiday and Holy Thursday, Good Friday and Holy Saturday are observed by all business houses.

Now the two months midwinter holiday is over, and the schools are open. The public schools are housed in old buildings, and the rooms are gay with the work of the children. There are large gardens and swimming pools in the patios. The trouble is there are not enough schools. Attendance is supposed to be compulsory, up to the age of fourteen, but there are no truant officers to enforce attendance and one sees many children on the street who help their parents in their work, or who have not fit clothes to attend.

# Spring Festival in Mexico

4

L AST FRIDAY was the Friday of Sorrows, the day of the sorrows of the Blessed Virgin, and, though in the churches at the solemn high Masses celebrated, the people hid their faces in their rebozos and serapes and wept, in the early morning the day was celebrated as one of the most colorful fiestas of the year. Later, of course, there would be joy and happiness too.

The government, regarding the will of the people, makes holidays of these holy days. The period from the Friday of Sorrows through Easter is called the Spring Festival, and advertised in the newspapers and on billboards about the town as such. But the government does not succeed in making people disregard the religious significance of the days. The churches are full.

The fiesta begins at five in the morning at Santa Anita on the Viga Canal which goes from Xochimilco Lake into the city. Every morning boats bring into Mexico City vegetables and flowers, but this day booths were erected in the fields all along the canal for several miles, merry-go-rounds, dancing pavilions, Ferris wheels and open air restaurants were set up, and business began at five.

It was very cold as we left our apartment in the city and drove out to Santa Anita, which is only a mile or so away from the center of town. The city streets were deserted and we thought that no one was up yet.

Originally published in *Commonweal*, July 16, 1930. Vol. XII, 296–7.

But when we got to Santa Anita there were literally thousands and thousands of people from the city, and the cobbled streets of the little puebla were so jammed with cars and trucks of people that it was impossible to move any further in the cab, so we got out to walk. As everyone else did, we bought wreaths of flowers and garlands to hang around our necks, made of gladiola blossoms of delicious colors. Then we sat down at a wayside restaurant for a breakfast of tamales, pancakes and coffee. The pancakes were impossible but the tamales were delicious and there were sweet ones for Teresa, so that her breakfast was just as good as though she had had sensible corn meal mush. Everyone else was eating mole (which is stewed turkey in a heavy spiced sauce), tamales made with chicken and chile, enchilades, tortillas, salads and beer. There was much dancing and riding on merry-go-rounds and Ferris wheels—this at six o'clock in the morning!

One of the customs of the fiesta is to buy eggs that have been emptied, colored, filled with water and covered with heavy gilt paper pasted over the top, and to crash these on your companions' heads. The eggs are thrown, too, like confetti. Another thing everyone buys is a little wooden boat with a wax man and woman in national costume, surrounded by beautifully colored wax vegetables—the cabbages, cauliflowers, squashes, radishes and lettuce, very large in proportion to the figures. The radishes here are both small and large, the latter over a foot long and several inches thick. The men selling the little wooden boats, which are mounted on a stick, have them all stuck in one large radish and the effect is very gay. Everyone was carrying bunches of small radishes with their bouquets of flowers, and eating them as they walked along.

People of every class attend this fiesta at Santa Anita. There were the Indians from the surrounding pueblas, sitting along the canal and selling their wares, middle-class Mexican families with their many children, charros on horseback, women with poblana dresses glittering with sequins, and many soldiers and officers with their girls. The richer (I do not like to say the better) class remained in their closed cars and looked out upon the scene.

One has a peculiar dissipated feeling after an early morning fiesta of this sort. Gaiety is more natural to us Anglo-Saxons in the evening. So it was with the proper subdued feeling that I assisted at the ten o'clock Mass in honor of Our Lady of Sorrows. The church was packed, so crowded that people were sitting on the foot of the altar rail, on every inch of the floor and on the steps of all the other altars around the church. I sat on the Gospel side of the altar of San Antonio, just where the feet of the priest had worn the carpet thin. Babies who were not yet able to crawl and were in no danger of rolling down the steps, were laid at the foot of the altar to kick blissfully throughout the long service.

That afternoon, Soledad, Teresa and I went to the country for the rest of the holiday. My little stone house in Xochimilco has a thatched roof, and geraniums, roses and cactus grow over the walls which bound my ten acres on two sides. On the other two sides there is the lagoon, where my funny flat-bottomed boat is tied to the bank. There is only one door and one window in the house so that it is dusky and cool and I must write outside with my typewriter propped up on a stone wall where melons and squashes are ripening in the sun.

We have finished our morning's work, or rather we have finished what we were allowed to do. As Soledad has an unfortunate habit of dropping half the dishes to the bottom of the lagoon, or breaking them by scrubbing them too vigorously, I wash the dishes while she cleans house. In the midst of it, Señora Torres, my landlady, came and took the escobeta out of my hand and refused to allow me to continue. "My pleasure," she kept insisting. It was my pleasure too, but she could not understand that. People hereabouts think it most scandalous that a stranger should do her own work. If she can afford to pay ten dollars a month for a house (three times what they consider it to be worth) and two fifty for a boat, surely she should have enough servants to do her work for her. So Señora Torres, who comes at seven every morning with the milk and eggs, sweeps out the patio, picks a bowl of flowers for me and insists on helping unless I hide the dishes until after she goes. When they are washed—they are of Mexican wear, the color of terra cotta, but shiny—they are hung on the outside wall of the house in the sun. Most people do their cooking, too, over a tin charcoal stove, but we are more luxurious and have an oil stove.

On our way to the plaza to do the day's marketing there is a little chapel of Santa Crucita, another of San Christobel and then the big parish church facing the market. We usually stop there for a moment and I watch with enjoyment Soledad's endeavor to teach Teresa to cross herself in the Mexican way. Here the large sign of the cross is made first, then traced on the forehead, the mouth and the breast, and then the large sign of the cross again. Sometimes this is repeated three times in honor of the Blessed Trinity, or of Jesus, Mary and Joseph. It looks, at first, a long and complicated process. At the end, one kisses one's hand which has traced the sacred sign. The sign of the cross is the most natural gesture of these people. Religion is part of their life. It is not just of pious people I am writing. It is of the majority, 80 or 90 percent of the people in Mexico.

On Palm Sunday Soledad and I attended Mass at the parish church, which is as large as the church of St. Francis Xavier in New York. It was crowded to suffocation, the Mass was long and wearisome, and worst of all I had left my missal in the city and had only a tiny prayerbook which omitted the Epistle and Gospel of the day. Nevertheless, it was a tremendously uplifting and glorious spectacle, and my eyes were filled with tears often. All the people had palms. Not palms such as we have in New York, but palms braided and plaited and woven into crosses, little altars, long plumes and the semblance of stalks of flowers, and interwoven with flowers of every color and delicious odor. Most of the palms were six feet tall, so the church was like a field of wheat, blossoming with flowers, waving and stirring triumphantly. When the priests went up to the altar, the people raised their palms on high so that one could see only the palms and the dark, gleaming faces of the Mexicans, uplifted like the palms, radiant. It seemed impossible, but the procession was able to pass through the church to the rear, and out the side doors. Then after a long interval, while the organ played, the huge doors, fifteen feet high, opened, letting in a flood of sunlight. At the doors three life-sized figures of Christ, one crowned with thorns, one after His scourging, and one carrying His cross, a grim reminder of what was to come, met the incoming procession. I wondered, as the Mass went on, how these people could celebrate the Resurrection of Christ more gloriously than they did this day of His triumphal entry into Jerusalem.

~

I wrote the above at ten o'clock this Easter Monday morning and then the church bells began ringing so merrily and the firecrackers in the plaza, which had awakened us at dawn, became so noisy that I had to venture out to see what the celebration was all about.

We had spent three hours on Good Friday in a sad gloomy church, and Easter Sunday we had attended the high Mass, which as I had expected, was nowhere near as glorious as that of Palm Sunday. And now it was Monday and the cobbled roads and paths across fields to the church were filled with gayly dressed Indians, children in pink and blue satin, the men in white cotton and linen colored blouses. All the seats in the church were taken and we had to find a place for ourselves on the floor as usual. In a few minutes, to gay and joyful music, the three priests came out in their white and gold robes, and showers of blossoms of all kinds began to float down through the church in steadily increasing density. The Mass was being said at the altar of the black Christ, blacker by far than any of the Indians in the congregation. During the Gloria in Excelsis little Indian boys appeared at windows high up above the altars, looking like cherubs painted there, and came to life to hurl down handfuls of roses and poppies which fell softly before the altar. The steady storm of blossoms was coming from five other apertures in the domes of the church.

For once Teresa was perfectly happy to sit through the long service. She got directly beneath the falling blossoms at the back of the church and she and a little Indian boy swept the petals around them into piles and tossed blossoms at each other gleefully. The music was very gay. There were violins, violas and flutes beside the organ, and I strongly suspect grand opera music was being played. Through all the Mass petals of carnations, violets, roses and poppies and shreds of calla lilies came floating through the air, falling on everyone, until the flowers were so heaped up around us that there was actually a wet sound of falling petals.

Sunday is a day in Xochimilco when every man, woman and child works, the women selling food and flowers, and the men and boys poling picnickers along the lagoons, and I wondered if this were the reason for the lavish celebration of Easter Monday. Coming out after Benediction, I tried to find out, asking in my Mexico City Spanish which is hard for these Indians to understand. One small boy said, "It is the feast of Christo Rey." Another said, "It is the Pascua." And a nice old Indian, who could not understand my questions about the black Christ, told me it was the Monday of Poppies and the feast of the Resurrection too.

# Bed

# 5

TERESA, FOUR AND A HANDFUL, sat at the library table with her crayons and paper in front of her and tried to ignore the fact that it was getting dark outside and that it was time for her to go to bed.

I sat at my desk trying to write letters.

"Here is a picture of a man, a man dancing and telling a whole lot of stories. He's playing on his catarrh too, and singing songs. Are you listening?"

"That's a lovely picture, darling," absent-mindedly.

"And here is a little boy, and he stays out in the garden all day, not in the house any more, because people are naughty to him. *Lookit!*"

"Uh-huh."

"*Lookit!*"

"Yes, I see, sweetheart."

"And this is just a man, *muy feo, muy feo. Muy grande boca, muy grande* ears, *asi,* and tomorrow I'll make three of four ears on him. Isn't he a terrible man? *Are you looking?*"

Teresa's conversation as well as her pictures were influenced by her recent stay in Mexico.

"And this is a kitchen with all the dishes hanging on the walls, and here is the Holy Ghost and there's fire-crackers in the kitchen and a fiesta. It's so much noise, I must go outside and play with the childuns.

Originally published in *Commonweal,* May 27, 1931. Vol. XIV, 100–1.

And the Virgin Mary is out there too with a little tiny baby, and this is a picture of me dancing, and the Virgin Mary is dancing too and there are leaves all around. *Do you hear me?*"

The clock struck eight.

"I don't wanna go to bed! I don't wanna go to bed!"

"But you have to go to bed, so come on, honey, and I'll help you unfasten."

"I can do it myself. Lemme do it myself!"

Then one of those hectic half-hours which mothers know. The bath; the shower, insisted upon to top it off; the splashing all over the bathroom floor; the desire, combated, to mop it up; the giving of the eight drops of concentrated cod liver oil, treated by violet ray, guaranteed to put on eight pounds a week, an elixir of life (only maybe it is the orange juice in which it is given which does the trick); the nightly battle over whether to wear "jamas" or a "nightie"; the insistence on the box of chessmen under the bed to wake up on in the morning.

Then prayers, repeated after me, begun in a kneeling posture, continued in a sitting, relapsing finally into some sort of gymnastic posture.

"*Teresa!*"

"What!" in pained surprise.

"Either sit down or kneel down, but for goodness' sake keep still."

"Won't the Virgin Mary like it if I try to stand on my head?"

Unanswerable question. I'm sure she does like it, but what is one to say?

"Now come on, hurry up and finish."

"I don't want to hurry up," piously. Teresa continued with a long list of people and things to be blessed by God, and then with a virtuous sense of duty done, she hopped into bed.

"What about a kiss?" she asked coyly.

"Here is a kiss." But it was too definite a one.

"I want lots of them."

"Mm-m. Lots."

"I want tickle kishes. Tickly kishes in the neck."

"There now, that's enough," very firmly.

"But I wanna drink o' water."

"Here."

"Lookit. A little moss in the glass of water." The little moth which had flown in from the garden just to complicate matters, was dumped down the wash-bowl.

"Did you throw it away?"

"Yes."

"Is it dead?"

"Uhuh."

"Did it get drowned?"

"Probably, and now for goodness' sake go to sleep."

"But I can't. I can't stop laughing. I'm laughing because Ernest was an elephunt. Isn't it funny that Ernest was an elephunt? I'm going to laugh and laugh until I have hiccups. Then you'll have to bring me another glass of water. All night long, you'll have to bring me a glass of water."

I have held Milne's poem of Mary Jane and her "rice pudding for supper again" against him, and now I was beginning to resent his famous elephant which was causing all the giggles.

The small voice rambled on. From the sitting-room I could hear it as it was intended I should.

"Doddee! Are you listening? I want to tell you a story. Once there was a little mouse and a bunny rabbit and the bunny had jamas on and a pretty little hat and he went to the mouse's house for supper and they had bumana and puddum for supper."

The story went on. The requests for attention went on.

"Are you listening to me? Why don't you answer me? I'm not going to sleep. Do you hear that I'm not going to sleep? Why didn't you tell me the story of Old Mother Cupboard who lived in a shoe and had so many childuns she didn't know what to do with them all? And what did Humpty Dumpty fall off the wall for? Was he a naughty boy and did his mama tell him not to climb up? You didn't cut out any paper dolls for me tonight. You didn't let me color the paper dolls that you didn't cut out. You didn't let me—"

There was no end to the things I had not let Teresa do that evening and which she wanted to do besides sleep.

"I want my doll in bed with me. Do you hear me?"

Feeling somewhat guilty by my child's recriminations, I got up and fetched her favorite doll.

"I'm going to tell my doll on you. You wouldn't let me—"

The small accusing voice continued. . . . And then—suddenly I realized that I had been reading for five or ten minutes in complete silence. Once more the nightly miracle had been accomplished. Teresa had fallen asleep.

# Now We Are Home Again            6

---

FOR TWO LONG SUMMERS I have been away from my little house on the shore of the island. We had rented it to friends and had gone traveling and working elsewhere. Now we are home again, Teresa and I, to find the garden overgrown with weeds, my perennials strangely distributed around the neighborhood and no longer in my own flower-beds, fish-lines and ten-foot poles strung around the room, a box of dead and dried worms and clams left under a couch on the back porch, and fish-hooks stored on the little shelf over the door where a cross used to be and where now a giant spider crab hangs on the wall.

The crucifix had been moved and hung in the attic, which Teresa and I make our sleeping quarters, and in the bustle of spring cleaning and homecoming I did not transfer it to its usual place for some weeks. In those weeks the rain poured down, the wind howled dismally around the house, I sprained my knee digging clams, Teresa had another attack of malaria, I was tormented with poison ivy, three short stories were turned down by magazines and in general life was dismal.

One evening as Teresa was getting ready for bed and knelt to say her prayers, she turned around to the shelf over which the ugly, but biologically interesting, specimen hung.

"There is no cross there," she said, "so I'll just say my prayers to the spider crab."

Originally published in *Commonweal*, August 19, 1931. Vol. XIV, 382–3.

Then and there we delayed the going to bed until the shelf had been nicely dusted, a little rose-studded shawl from Mexico hung over it, and the crucifix brought down from the attic and a few hyacinths from the garden placed in front of it.

We both slept very well that night, in spite of the howling of the wind which sounded like devils battering against the little house. I can laugh at myself for my Irish forebodings, but I believe in devils as I do in angels. I have heard them before in the gloomy melancholy of the wind and have felt that I have had a glimpse of hell in a sudden knowledge of the horror of the absence of God. I have felt a devil in the shape of a little fly which buzzed about my ear as I walked two miles home on a hot summer afternoon, after I had been gossiping with a friend about a neighbor.

But now with the spider crab hanging from a nail over the dining-room table in its proper place, the sun has come out, Teresa is better, my poison ivy is gone, my young brother has his first job on the country paper, I have been given work for the summer in the way of garden interviews, and life is serene and happy once more.

The island is ten miles long and four miles wide and, although there is a railroad running from one end of it to another, it would be necessary to walk miles and miles to interview the members of the horticultural clubs. So though my salary did not warrant it, I have bought myself a car. It is eight years old and it cost only $35.00. But with license plates, new tires, and the things that needed adjusting such as the carburetor, coils, wires, etc., I found that within a couple of weeks I had paid $75.00, all told. Now it is running smoothly and Teresa and I whirl around the country roads at a dizzying speed (twenty miles an hour) and stop off at old farmhouses and beautiful estates and dingy, little new houses and bright and shining new houses, and talk to their occupants about flowers.

We find people raising other things too: alligators, large ones, in little green houses; bull frogs in fish pools; newts and salamanders in terrariums; turtles, birds, rabbits, even snakes. Teresa thinks my job is great fun, especially since she is often presented with flowers and plants for her own little garden, and other things, such as a parasol, and a kitten!

She had long wanted a kitten but we had been traveling around so much that it was impossible to keep one. It is true we had two little ones in Xochimilco, Mexico. We got them when we were living in our stone house with the thatched roof, to scare away the field mice which ran across the bed at night. The kittens didn't do much good. We locked them in at night, but in the morning they used to run back to the Indian's wattle hut next door where there was a fat pig and several turkeys, both alive and in the shape of *mole* plentifully spiced with peppers, to keep them company, inside and out.

But our kitten here is very much with us. He thinks his tray of sand is to play in, and he jumps in and out, scattering sand all around, hunting for an occasional pebble. When I cuffed him the other day for a misdemeanor—very cold-bloodedly, for I was in a happy humor and only meant to remind him that some things aren't done—Teresa looked at me with astonishment.

"You made my eyes get swampy when you did that to my little cat," she said reproachfully.

It is fun to get in the car and go jouncing along to see new places and people, and both the places and people are very nice, having to do with flowers and birds and beasts as they do. We jump and leap occasionally, "like a goat" Teresa says, but generally the car runs smoothly. Once we got stuck on the side of Grymes Hill, where Maxim Gorki and Dickens visited when they were here. (Little is known about their stay.) It is a very steep hill, and I bore down on the foot brake so hard that my sprained knee started hurting grievously.

"We just can't do anything," Teresa said in her resigned way, "so we'll just admire the scenery." We were concentrating on this when a truck came along and nosed us up to the top very kindly.

We never telephone people we are coming, because the nicest ones are the quiet ones who don't like to be interviewed, and we find that it serves better just to walk in on them and trust to luck that they will be hospitable and talkative about their plants. Mrs. Stirn, a nice old German woman, was a pleasant refuge to us after our strain and excitement of getting there, and we sat on her terrace looking out over the Narrows, and talked of Capri and Axel Munthe and many other things besides flowers, while Teresa tried to catch a little snake which had clumsily fallen down out of the rock garden into a tiny pool of water which was made there for birds and rabbits.

Our own garden is not doing so very well. The soil is full of clay which hardens like cement; the five pounds of grass seed which I sowed have been blown away or eaten by the starlings, and what is left is coming up in a most haphazard manner. But the irises which used to form a hedge around the house and are now in clumps, are bursting into flower, and the forsythia is blooming like bursts of sunshine around the house. Just beyond my little lawn and the wild cherry and apple trees, the ground dips sharply to the sands, which are as yellow and as warm as ever. The bay is a calm gray blue today, and the little waves chuckle along the beach.

Every afternoon we lie in the sun there and keep very still to hear the last of the gulls who are on their way further north for the summer and to listen to the water and the land birds. Sometimes Lefty, who has a vocation for poverty, comes out of his shack, where he lives winter and summer, and skins eels and washes clams for his supper and keeps us company. He does not like money, nor need it, and lives by exchange, bringing a mess of fish to the barber for a haircut and digging worms for fishermen in exchange for groceries and loaning out his boat for kerosene to fill his lamp. He heats and cooks in his little shack by a driftwood fire.

Down in Mexico I had the endless lagoons of Xochimilco on every side, with the mountains rising up around them. Here are the long reaches of the bay. Down there I was surrounded by a garden full of violets, roses, cactus flowers, calla-lilies and pomegranate trees, but never a blade of grass. Here is green, lush green, everywhere.

Down there in the country I lived in a house where the doors and windows were of solid oak and had to be taken down in the morning to let light into the place. It is a land which cannot afford glass windows in the country places. But here there are six windows looking out on the meadows, the sands and the bay.

I am very glad to be home again, to be cultivating my own bit of soil, to be living in my own house and to feel, for the time at least, that I am never going to leave it again. There is beauty here too, a lovely, gentle beauty of cultivated gardens and woodlands and shore. We picked flowers the other day in the woods—dogwood, wild lily of the valley, quince blossoms, blueberry blossoms and the last of the violets. Along the road we gathered sweet clover to put in the hot attic, where its fragrance will be distilled and fill the house, and Teresa sighed happily, "Flowers and grass and things are so beautiful, they just hurt my feelings."

# Notes from Florida

7

YOUNG TERESA AND I have moved our place of residence again and are visiting my mother in Florida. Florida is like the garden of Eden, and "Let us stay here always," Teresa says.

It is not a Catholic country—as Mexico or even New York, is Catholic. There are only four Catholic churches in Miami and the vicinity. One is in Coral Gables, three miles away from our house. This Church of the Little Flower is set in the midst of oleander, mango and grapefruit trees. On the next block to it is a large coeducational school in charge of the Sisters of St. Joseph, and here Teresa goes to school. In the kindergarten (Teresa is now five) the children learn to read and write and do simple sums. Teresa has been going to school for a month now and can read four pages of her primer.

As I write, big black storm clouds are rising in the south. To the east, through the open French doors, the sky is delft blue with little feathery clouds. The Florida pines rear their plumed masts to the sky, and under them, dotting the open fields, are seedling pines, bright green. There is a heavily wooded hummock at the end of the road, and only one house in sight, surrounded by scarlet crotons and a field of tomato plants. The sun comes from behind the clouds, shining brilliantly, but there is always the noise of the wind which has kept up now for months. Everyone says, "In September or October, the hurricane season, we would all be worried to hear such continuous wind."

Originally published in *Commonweal*, June 22, 1932. Vol. XVI, 212–13.

A quarter of a mile away is Coconut Grove, the colored town, where the little frame houses are so thickly surrounded by royal poinciana, strangler fig, mango, orange, grapefruit and other low-growing trees, that one can scarcely see them. Over-topping the other trees are banana palms and coconut palms. Most of the colored churches are called Churches of God, and on Sunday nights we often hear the gay singing from the nearest of them. We stopped one night and sat outside to listen, and I was sorry that I did not have Teresa with me to see the little girls dancing back and forth with babies in their arms.

I saw nothing to repel me there as one often is repelled at camp meetings of white people. It was a song meeting pure and simple, and occasionally the singers would get down on their knees, burying their faces in the seats of their chairs. One fat old woman dressed all in white called out, "Praise God cause Ise got salvation." An old gray-haired Negro echoed her. A little girl piped up, "Praise Jesus for coming and saving us." And others called out their thanks.

Then someone started a hymn and the piano, the drums, the tambourines, the shuffling feet, the clapping hands, and the voices of men, women and children took it up. The rafters rang as the worshipers sang and danced. It was gay!

Toto is the old colored woman who works for my mother. Two weeks ago her eighteen-year-old daughter, Evelina—one of eight children—died. My mother and three other ladies for whom Toto works, went to the funeral on the following Sunday. It was held in the little Spanish-style Episcopal church down on Hibiscus Avenue. The gowned minister, the little boys with censers, the leader of the choir carrying the cross, and the choir of men and women and little boys waited outside under the mango trees until the funeral procession came down the street. The white coffin was covered with flowers, and on either side walked men in black and girls in white, carrying wreaths of real and artificial flowers. Then came Toto dressed all in black, with a black crepe veil; her husband, a skilled mechanic and son of a white man; Frank and John who work as housemen; Alfred who is married; the two little boys, R. J. and Eli; and the one remaining daughter, who is married, and her five children.

They all entered the church, which was filled to overflowing. The singing was impressive, the deep bass voices of the men in the choir booming out all over the church. The service went on with quiet dignity until after the sermon, when the choir was again singing. Night was falling outside. All day the sky had been an indigo blue, and intermittent

showers had laid the dust and intensified the tropic colors. Through
the deepening gloom of the church a wail started, a howling from Toto's
daughter who remained. Toto joined in, wailing too as she swung back
and fourth, swaying in her anguish.

When I came downstairs at seven the next morning, Toto was light-
ing the pine-log fire in the field to boil the clothes. She had not eaten
nor slept for two nights and days but she wanted to work: it was a relief, she said. When I put a big lunch in front of her at noon, I sat talking to her so that she would forget she was eating and the food would
not choke her.

All the Saturday night that Evelina died, they sang, Toto said, as
they sat around her bed. There was Frankie, her most loved brother;
her father; the minister from the church; and her two little brothers,
R. J. and Eli. Every now and then R. J. and Eli went out to nibble at the
fudge which I had sent over to Evelina the week before. The tuberculosis
had gone to her throat and she had said that it helped, to suck on the
sweet candy. But she would not want it any more, R. J. and Eli thought,
and they had been very considerate before.

Toto sat out on the dark porch. Overhead the moon flickered through
the leaves of the poinciana trees, and the rustling of the dried pods of the
tree, which hung in yellow festoons during the day, sounded like the
clapping of many hands.

Each time she went into the house, into the bedroom just inside the
door, Evelina said, "Have you given me up yet, mother?" And Toto
said, "No. I can't give you up."

Then Evelina said, "Go and talk to the Lord, mother, and see if you
can't give me up. You are keeping me here and I want to go." So Toto
went out on the porch again and sat in the cold moonlight and talked to
God.

Finally when she went in, Evelina said, "Mother, have you given me
up?" And Toto said, "Yes, child, I have given you up to the Lord." And
so Evelina went to sleep, and in her sleep she died.

As I listened to Toto talking of Evelina, and of the children who are
left to her, I thought of the dense gloom of that little porch, which is in
reality but a platform since the porch blew away during the hurricane
of 1926. I thought of the over-hanging trees, of the seventeen avocado
trees which Toto's children had planted around the house. I thought of
the happiness that little house has seen and the misery it now contains.
I thought of those night hours on the porch, and I heard again that
awful wailing in the church. "But it is God's will," Toto said, getting up

from the table, her eyes strong and shining. And she went back to her ironingboard set up outside in the western sun.

# East Twelfth Street  8

W HEN WE CAME BACK to New York from our visit to Florida, Teresa and I, we had an opportunity to rent our little summer place for six months, so we were faced with the necessity of finding a home for ourselves and furniture to put in it. Hotel bills being exhorbitant, we were in a rush, and in a few days we found a comfortable tenement apartment, with steam heat, hot water and plenty of sunlight—all for $28.00 a month, in the warmly crowded neighborhood of Avenue A and Twelfth Street. It was early spring with a cold tang in the air, very refreshing after the torpid heat of Florida. We had both sunlight and warmth, and best of all, a huge expanse of sky to look out upon, owing to the presence of a long low garage on the other side of the street. Every night we could watch the sky in the south change from rose to violet, and as the spring advanced, there were the early storms to enjoy, massive clouds, pierced by lances of lightning, sheets of silver rain against the purple dusk. It is a luxury indeed to have acres of sky to look out upon in New York City.

"We have the two most important things right on our street," said Teresa, thinking of the miles we had to go in Florida to reach a church. "You can go to Mass every day and leave me home to play, and I can go to school and leave you home to work. I don't need to go to church, do I, because we have plenty of praying in school? Too much sometimes."

Originally published in *Commonweal*, November 30, 1932. Vol. XVII, 128–9.

The school, which was one she had attended before, is a day nursery just down the street, run by the Helpers of the Sacred Heart. Babies of one year old and up are taken care of, children of the first three grades are taught, and the children who have passed on to higher grades and are attending other schools, public and parochial, in the neighborhood, come back to the nursery for their luncheon and for after-school activities. There are 275 children taken care of all day long by the Sisters, in addition to the children who come in for meals. The place is large and roomy, and there is a roof garden and a backyard and a play-room under the roof for recreation.

One of the Sisters of the order heads a Sunday School too, which takes care of 1,200 young ones in the district who attend public school.

"Today," said Teresa, "I had four dishes of spaghetti. It was very good."

"It must have been."

"There was one little boy who had six. But he was a *cochina*. He is always hungry. Every afternoon after school when we have bread and jam or bread and cheese—if it's bread and cheese, I give him the cheese."

Lunch is not confined to spaghetti alone. Perhaps there is pineapple or stewed apricots for dessert. And bread and milk too.

The nursery is open from seven in the morning until six at night, and children are cared for all day and fed practically two meals a day for $1.20 a week.

At this time, where there is great talk about provision made for the babies and little children by the Soviet government, it is good to call attention to the fact that Mother Church has always kept in mind the pre-school child. There are nurseries in every section of the city for the child of the working mother. The state and city, except for clinics, have always ignored the needs of the child under kindergarten age, and those attending kindergarten are only cared for three hours a day. What other nurseries there are, are either very expensive affairs, charging from $30.00 to $75.00 a month, or else works of charity, run by brisk social workers for the "lower classes."

Little Teresa attended one of these her first and second winters, and I shall never forget the painted chairs on which the little ones sat and sat, and the painted toys (to be looked at) on the shelves, and the uniforms covering the heterogeneous garments of the poor, and the briskness, the terrible briskness, of those in charge. I remember coming early to the nursery one winter afternoon, in time to get a glimpse of child after child being propelled with horrid speed in and out of the washroom, and the worn and haggard faces of the attendant looking forward to the end of the day. Thank God, the Sisters think in terms of eternity. There is never that unpleasant hurry.

The church across the street from us is an Italian church, and there are dramatic funerals very often, with a band accompanying the hearse down the street to the church. The automobiles move along at a funereal pace, the band, when it is not playing, drags its many feet with a shushing along the asphalt, and as the cortege approaches, the bell from the church tower tolls a single spaced note, a dread and mournful sound. The music is triumphant and soul-stirring, lending an especial poignance to the spectacle.

To Teresa, this glimpse of death with its massed flowers, its dignity and solemnity, has lent a new aspect to heaven. A year ago she had said, "I do not want to die and go to heaven. I want to stay where there is plenty of fresh air." And this evident impression of a stuffy heaven which she had in some way or other visualized, dismayed me. She was thinking of the grave, I assured her, and not of a heaven which was filled with not only all the present delights of her life, but many more.

"Beaches?" she wanted to know. "And many little crabs and snails and pretty shells? I do want to live on a beach in heaven." And I assured her that there were indeed beaches in heaven.

The brass band and flowers of the Italian funerals lent emphasis in some way to my recital of heavenly joys and she said contentedly that if either of us got there first, we would wait for the other.

Along the side walls of the church are glass-enclosed statues: Our Lady of the City, Our Lady of Perpetual Help, Our Lady of Grace, Our Lady of Mt. Carmel, Our Lady, Help of Christians and Our Lady of Lourdes. In addition to the usual statues of Saint Joseph, Saint Anthony, Saint Thérèse and Saint Anne, there are those of Cosmos and Damien, Saint Sebastian, a fine figure of Saint John the Baptist dressed in real sheepskin, and Blessed Don Bosco in a little shrine all his own.

There was a tremendous procession which stretched for ten blocks around the church on the feast day of Our Lady, Help of Christians, and though the day was cold, there was a line of white-clad girls wreathed and garlanded and carrying banners. It was impressive to see the older women, bent and twisted by life, holding aloft the banners of their faith, on which were emblazoned the insignia of the associations and confraternities to which they belonged. . . .

As I mentioned before, there was not only the problem of finding a home, but furniture to fill it, since all my belongings were in the country. I was able to bring in two beds, my sister contributed chairs and a table, other contributions were forthcoming in the shape of wicker furniture, pillows, rugs, etc., and my younger brother, whom we sometimes call Brother Juniper, insisted upon making me some furniture. His bookcases looked solid until books were put into them, and then they teetered dangerously. His benches could not be sat on. The table he constructed for my typewriter looked so heavy and solid that I was deceived into a feeling of security about it and began using it at once.

It is my custom when possible to attend Benediction. ("I am perficky able to mind the house and take care of myself," Teresa says.) So one evening, on coming in at eight thirty, I was startled to hear shrieks and wails of neighbors coming from my front room. I sped up the stairs, with my heart pounding, and found Brother Juniper's table in pieces on the floor, and my typewriter and papers in wild confusion all around. Teresa and Anita, the little girl next door, had merely bumped into it and the table had gone down.

My neighbor with Jewish emotionalism had rushed to the rescue and, seeing that it was my means of livelihood which had fallen on the floor, and fearing that her child had had some part in the desecration of my desk, she had started her wailings which had brought the whole house to my door.

Little Anita was Teresa's constant playmate after school all through the spring. Not old enough to go to school herself, she insisted on coming in to play school, or "Make for fun you're my baby and I'm your mama," was one of the games. Anita is very tiny, with long hair which hangs in pigtails on either side of her fat face. She and Teresa were very fond of each other, and it was hard to drag them apart at bedtime.

"Let me stay just until she gets into bed," Anita said.

"Let her stay just until I say my prayers," Teresa added.

And this custom of letting Anita stay made Teresa forget that sometimes there were too many prayers and that some of them were too long. I myself did not know how many prayers she knew until she used them all as a means of letting Anita stay, and then I heard, for the first time, the Creed, the Acts of Contrition, of Charity and of Hope, in addition to the Lord's Prayer and the Hail Mary. When the bless-thems came along, Anita waited with breathless interest until her name too was mentioned among the friends and relatives.

It was Anita who started the game of "Make for fun we are two ladies with lots of little babies and we must go to visit the Lady Mary." So they sat with their doll carriages beneath the statue on the mantelpiece and talked of tonsilectomies and feedings, while the figure of Our Lady of Grace, which has been blessed by a Pope and has traveled from Rome to Spain, to South America, to New York, presided with a benign smile over two little girls of East Twelfth Street.

# Review:
# Everybody's Saint

# 9

Saint Elizabeth *by Elisabeth von Schmidt-Pauli. New York: Henry Holt and Company. $2.50.*

THE LOVE OF HER HUSBAND LOUIS, the true friendship of Ysentrud and Guda, and her own love for her three little children—all these the Hungarian Princess Elizabeth gave up or was forced to give up in her search for perfection. Beside these bonds of human love, the wealth she renounced was as nothing. Most of the emphasis in this account of Saint Elizabeth is laid upon the worldly honors and splendor she renounced, and perhaps that is because in drawing a faithful picture of the luxurious age in which she lived, the author felt this background and description to be necessary.

The love story of Louis and Elizabeth is more detailed in treatment, and the reader is given a charming picture of Louis as a brave knight, whose love for God and striving for individual salvation warred with his love for the Emperor Frederick, and of Elizabeth as a loving wife and mother. Her love was so strong, "that all her love of other people and things was illumined more by her personal happiness than by the light of God," the author says. But when Louis died, Elizabeth was free to give up all and follow in the footsteps of Saint Francis of Assisi who had bequeathed her his cloak to wear. When the dour Magister Conrad

Originally published in *Commonweal*, December 28, 1932. Vol. XVII, 250.

comes into the story, and Elizabeth, Ysentrud and Guda, the three faithful friends, strive to obey his harsh precepts, the story becomes most interesting.

Saint Elizabeth's life has the charm of that of the Little Flower, and though differing in a great many ways, they yet are strangely alike. Both were gay and happy in their service, and childlike in their trust and faith. Both died at the age of twenty-four and were canonized shortly after death. Both worked miracles immediately after death.

The Little Flower left us her story with its intimate details as to the life of her soul. Elisabeth von Schmidt-Pauli's book makes us anxious to read the letters sent by Saint Elizabeth's stern advisor Conrad to Pope Gregory IX and the testimony of her female attendants taken by the papal commission.

# Real Revolutionists                    **10**

---

O N THE SAME DAY that the unemployed hunger marchers were being ushered out of the city of Washington by the entire police force of the capital, with machine guns, tear gas bombs and nauseating gas bombs, a delegation of 250 farmers from twenty-six states were being welcomed to the city with every show of courtesy.

And on the same day too, machine guns and tear gas were being used out in Elkton, Wisconsin, to evict a farmer, his wife and two children from a farm which they were defending with rifles and shotguns. The home of the farmer, Max Cichon, had been sold at a foreclosure last August, and he had refused to move. It is evictions such as these that the farmers came to protest.

"We are not coming to Congress with our hats in our hands asking them to please do something for us," one of the delegates said. "We are going to demand aid, and if we don't get it, we are gong to resort to united and direct action. We are drawing up a declaration of independence just as was done back in 1776. Now we are fighting not one king, but many. We have to fight the banks, the lumber trusts, the insurance companies, the food trusts, the railroads and the milk trusts. The old American army fought without uniforms and without proper arms, and they were finally victorious. We are going to fight too."

The farmers' gathering was a happening of far more revolutionary significance than that of the hunger marchers. The hunger marchers

Originally published in *Commonweal*, January 11, 1933. Vol. XVII, 293–4.

were recruited by Communist leaders from the ranks of the unemployed, from union workers, from the textile mills, the mines and the factories. The majority of them not Communists, they had been trained for the past month or so in Communist language and tactics, and the demands they presented were but temporary panaceas for the evils of the depression. They were people who had lost all, who had nothing "but their chains to lose" as the Russian slogan has it. But the farmers, who have their farms and their living which they make on the farms to lose, are far more keen for the fight, and are far more apt to resort to immediate violence to gain their demands.

The conference met for four days, from December 7–11. The farmers present were delegates from their counties and states, elected either by their neighborhoods or by some organization such as the Farmers' Holiday Association, the Farmers' Union, the United Farmers' League, etc. Many of the men are former members of the old Non-Partizan League. The United Farmers' League is an organization with Communist affiliations, but it was estimated that not more than 5 percent of the farmers at the conference came from this organization.

I talked with one such representative, Selmen Espeland of Montana. All he thought of his organization was that it had specific demands which tallied with those of the more militant members of the rank and file farmers of the Farmers' Holiday Association. He said that he would join with any organization which was fighting for those demands. An emergency moratorium and a cessation of evictions and forced sales were the two measures which he thought the most important. And in the final statement read before Congress, the demands of the farmers went even farther. They embraced a cancellation of all "mortgages, interest, Food and Seed Loans and debts for supplies and furnishing for farmers whose volume of production and economic unit has always been too small to carry the debt of land and support the family at a minimum health standard (marginal farmers, share croppers and others)."

The moratorium was for all farmers "whose volume of production has until recently sustained the farm family at a decent standard of living."

In the demand that there shall be no more evictions from the farms, the statement reads, "If our duly elected national representatives fail as did the local, county and state authorities, then we pledge ourselves to protect our fellow farmers from suffering and their families from social disintegration by our united action."

From the floor of the union hall where the farmers met they did not hesitate to say what form that united action would take. Stump farmers from Minnesota, berry farmers from the Dakotas, maple sugar farmers from New Hampshire, cotton sharecroppers from Alabama, dairy farmers from Nebraska, corn, wheat, hog farmers—all dirt farmers—pledged themselves to go to the aid of any farmer in their county who was being menaced with dispossession.

"I'll defend my farm with shotguns," one farmer after another said. "And before I'm killed, I'll burn my crops, burn my house and poison my cattle. The farm is mine and I'll fight for it!"

These farmers are American radicals in the truest sense of the word. The majority of them, from the Farmers' Holiday Association, are men past forty, substantial in their home communities, church members, and up to the last few years not interested in social action. Those from Madison County, Nebraska, where in September of this year the resolution was taken to make the march on Washington, are Americans of Scandinavian, German or American descent, who have been Republicans for generations and who this year for the first time voted the Democratic ticket. In realizing their own predicament, they have begun to realize the plight of the industrial masses, and they do not hesitate to pledge themselves also to "united action" in the case of strikes and labor troubles in the towns near their farms, and this action in the form of mass gatherings and moral pressure has been brought to bear in the mining regions of Minnesota. The farmers have also cooperated with the striking miners in Illinois.

They cite the Golden Rule as the immediate solution of their difficulties but they hard-headedly state that "united militant action" will probably be necessary.

"We aim to avoid bloodshed," Anthony Rosenberg, the chairman of the convention, said. Rosenberg is a tall grizzled farmer of German descent (neither a Jew nor a New York radical, as has been suggested in reference to his name). "We come here to seek emergency legislation. But if nothing is done for us we will act on the conviction that the rights of the individual are above all man-made laws. The farmers' organizations are all endorsing our policy of direct action. Since September, after the governors' convention in Sioux City, Iowa, failed to do anything for us, we have organized the farmers in Nebraska so that now 9,000 of them belong to the Farmers' Holiday Association."

Alfred Tiala belongs to a farm organization in Minnesota. Dressed in khaki leggings, corduroy trousers and a leather jacket, he told how he had come across country with the hunger marchers. "We were both on our way to Washington and we joined forces. They are industrial workers and we are farmers, and our cause is the same. They tell us here in Washington to raise less crops—there is all this talk of surplus. And then we go through cities and see soup lines and starvation and realize that at home we have pigs we can't sell, wool we can't market and crops rotting in the ground. We have got to find some way to get this food to these starving workers."

Tiala's father and relatives, he said, worked on the Mesaba iron range, and when they were blacklisted years ago for joining the union, they hired out as farm hands, as many of the iron miners did. By heartbreaking work and frugality they saved until they bought their own farms. Now most of them have been dispossessed and the rest of them are subject to eviction shortly. Not far away from the industrial class themselves, they have sympathy with the city workers and bring in their supplies to swell the relief stores of the cities nearby.

This same relief work went on in southern Illinois during the strike this fall in the coal regions. The striking miners went out to the farms and helped bring in the crops and received payment in kind, which they put into a common fund of food for the needy in their mining towns.

Mrs. Ella Chase, a maple sugar farmer from New Hampshire, got up and made a stirring speech, her voice trembling with excitement.

"I worked for a week, cooking food for my five children so that I could come to Washington with my husband," she said. "They asked me why I was going. I told them I was going to fight so that they could live. I've been married for twenty years and my husband and I have worked from sixteen to twenty hours a day, and now we are in danger of being evicted, sold out. We've belonged to the grange and to the farm bureaus. We've joined all organizations trying to better the lot of the farmer. But this is the first time the farmers have united to actually fight. We've had a depression for ten years, we farmers, and we can't hold out. So we have to cooperate and fight evictions."

At an experience meeting men with names like Gore, Oliver, McCabe, Strong, all from the West, told of conditions in their communities. Philip Smith of Pennsylvania told how his forefathers had received their land by grant from Penn's sons. They were Americans all, and they professed themselves to be the real lovers of their country.

"The bankers, the insurance men, the railroad men—these are the real traitors," they said.

The demands which were drawn up and presented to Congress on the third day of the convention included, in addition to those mentioned before, $500,000,000 cash relief; food products needed for relief of the city workers to be purchased from the farmers; the transportation of relief supplies to be regulated by the federal government; a price-regulating body controlled by actual consumers and producers to make adjustment of prices; the defeat of any legislation based on the theory of "surplus" production, such as the Allotment Plan.

# Review:
# Catholic Poets

# 11

The Catholic Anthology *by Thomas Walsh; revised edition with additional poems selected by George N. Shuster. New York: The Macmillan Company. $2.50.*

AFTER GOING OVER the new poems in the revised edition of "The Catholic Anthology"—and a satisfactory list they are, too—I turned to the "Hound of Heaven," and I thought, as I read it over, of the first time I had heard it, recited almost entire by Eugene O'Neill, in the back room of an old-fashioned saloon (it was before prohibition) called the Golden Swan, a popular meeting place which used to be on the corner of Sixth Avenue and Fourth Street.

O'Neill was hanging around New York waiting for something to be done about his first full-length plays which were in the hands of Broadway producers. As yet he had achieved no popular success, but his one-act plays were being produced with gusto by the Provincetown Players around the corner. In the interminable waiting which goes on around a theatre, there was a good deal of time spent in the old saloon. There was a sliding window in the back room which led to a restaurant, so that one could wine and dine there after a fashion.

O'Neill used to sit there, glum and dour, and one night the talk turned on Francis Thompson. O'Neill knew almost all of his great poem, and leaning on the table, he searched his memory for it, and in his rather gritty, monotonous voice, he recited it with emotion. Indeed there was

Originally published in *Commonweal*, February 8, 1933. Vol. XVII, 415–16.

such force in his reading of the lines—it was as though he were reading them on the table before him—that many of them were impressed on my mind, never to be forgotten.

He was about thirty then, I think, and it was with melancholy joy that he remembered first that part of the poem:

> "In the rash lustihead of my young powers
>     I shook the pillaring hours
> And pulled my life upon me; grimed with smears,
> I stand amid the dust o' the mounded years—
> My mangled youth lies dead beneath the heap.
> My days have crackled and gone up in smoke,
> Have puffed and burst as sun-starts on a stream.
>         Yea, faileth now even dream
> The dreamer, and lute the lutanist;
> Even the linked fantasies, in whose blossomy twist
> I swung the earth a trinket at my wrist,
> Are yielding; cords of all too weak account
> For earth, with heavy griefs so overplussed."

It is good to pass on poems to others. An Irishwoman had given me those of Saint Patrick which are in the "Anthology," and I in turn had passed on Crashaw to a young Spanish radical whose saving grace is that she loves Saint Teresa and Saint John of the Cross; she in turn had presented me with translations of the two great Spanish saints.

When she dropped by this afternoon and laid hands on the "Anthology," she began reading aloud about Don John of Austria, shouting exuberantly (it is a poem which makes you shout) of her love for Chesterton.

"He is truly Spanish," she assured us, paying him the highest compliment in her power.

This collection containing all these poems shall go on my special shelf with the "Little Flowers of Saint Francis," "Confessions of Saint Augustine," "Autobiography and Foundations of Saint Teresa," and the "Jesuit Relations."

Since the feast day of the new American saints, I've been reading and rereading the last-named book, and today in the "Anthology" I found a fitting foreword to those brave letters from the saints.

It is part of a poem of Crashaw on the Holy Name, and should, I think, be dedicated to Isaac Jogues, John Brébeuf and their companions who:

　　　　　　. . . gave glorious chase
To persecutions, and against the face
Of death and fiercest dangers durst, with brave
And sober pace, march on to meet a grave!
On their bold breasts above the world they bore Thee,
And to the teeth of hell stood up to teach Thee,
In center of their inmost souls they wore Thee,
Where rack and torment strove in vain to reach Thee.

Aren't these fitting lines for those who died with the Holy Name on their lips?

# For the Truly Poor

# 12

MARIA HAS COME IN from the country where she has been living for the past years, and we are going out to look for an apartment for her. It is for herself, her two children and husband. Without money they could no longer get along in the country. The city offers Alan a job at $15.00 a week and now the problem is, finding a home. The family of four cannot live on $15.00 a week, you say? Nonsense! With courage and determination, one can do anything. Well, of course, if they are used to it. . . . But they are not. They are used to owning their own home, to having a car, to sending their children to a private school.

But Maria meets problems with a fine spirit and refuses to be defeated.

It is one of those keen, clear January days with a faint warmth in the air—a good day for a brisk walk. Starting south on Avenue A, we face a sharp wind and a dazzling winter sun which hangs low over the houses. It is early, only two o'clock in the afternoon, and it is amazing how much light and sparkle there is in that sun which hangs so low in the sky.

We have no set plan, Maria and I, that is to say, we do not really know where we are going to look. We are just setting out to walk up one street and down another until a likely place presents itself. Nevertheless, I more or less know what I am doing, for I have placed the whole matter in the hands of Saint Joseph. He is a fine one to find a home for you, I tell Maria.

Originally published in *Commonweal*, March 15, 1933. Vol. XVII, 544–5.

Maria is a Communist, but she is very fond of me, and if I think Saint Joseph is going to guide us, well and good.

He should be especially helpful, I add, since he had so much trouble himself in finding a place for Mary and the Child, and in consideration of the fact that we are modest in our demands, not expecting much more than a stable for the rent we can pay, he will surely guide us.

On 15th Street, just across from the Immaculate Conception Church, there is an empty flat. But though the outside of the building is clean, the inside is not, and the rent is exorbitant. Twenty dollars for four rooms, no heat, no hot water, no bath! Impossible. We are not being finicky, we just know we can do better.

As I say, we had no plan on setting out, but we did intend to confine our researches to one area—that large sprawling part of the East Side, bounded by Williamsburg Bridge on the south, 14th Street on the north, the East River and Avenue A. This is a section apart from subways and elevated trains and accessible only by meandering buses or crosstown cars, which means that to get anywhere you have to pay two fares. But Maria likes to walk and so does Alan, and he can get up a half an hour earlier to make the long crosstown hike and save carfare, and the walking will be enlivening and he won't miss the country so much.

We are finding the walk enlivening ourselves, and as we go, we peer through doorways, looking for backyard houses.

Did you know that all over the East Side there are hidden streets, accessible only through front buildings or obscure alleys, and on these hidden streets there are sometimes stables or little houses or rows of apartment buildings hidden from the world? These are quiet places, away from the noise of the street, away from trucks and taxis and street cars, and often, if the houses in front are high and those in back low, away from sunlight and air too. But sometimes the position is reversed, the houses in back are high and those in front low, and there is apt to be a bargain there.

One such place we found, back of Avenue A. It was a tall, slim backyard house, four stories high, an apartment to a story, and each apartment renting for $14.00 a month.

But the janitor's husband reeled at us dangerously, and the smell of alcohol sent us fleeing to the street.

We cut over through Tompkins Square, to get to Avenue B, and it was good to feel the spongy earth under foot, though the feel of it brought a nostalgia for the fields.

Down on 8th Street past Avenue C there was an old house (not a backyard house) facing north and south, with a trampled back yard. But the rooms were large and light and high-ceilinged, the house was a well-built one, and despite the neighborhood, which was teeming with children, one felt the luxury of space and nobly proportioned rooms. There were well-appointed bathrooms, good electric fixtures, a well-outfitted kitchen. But the rent for this place was too high, $25.00, and the gas bill would bring it up to $35.00, what with the heating of both house and water; and a man getting $15.00 a week cannot afford that, said Maria firmly.

Cutting across Avenue C which is a wide sunny street, we passed the pushcarts piled with artichokes, tomatoes, mushrooms and all kinds of fruits.

"A penny a piece for artichokes," I cried, buying some, "and mushrooms only fifteen a pound. One can always eat anyway."

"We got a letter from our cousin in Russia," Maria said, "and he writes that nowadays when the people talk about America they don't want to hear about our industries or high buildings, but about the food for sale on the pushcarts where all can buy. They say, 'Can you really buy all the bread and butter you can eat? Can you really have fresh fruits and meats? And it is cheap?' It is very sad."

We cut back along 7th Street toward the part where the school children are beginning to gather for play. This street is not as crowded as 11th, 12th or 13th. Those are supposed to be rough streets. Seventh Street has synagogues and women sitting out in the sun with baby carriages. On one side there is a public school. Around the corner on the square is St. Bridget's Church, with a parochial school in back.

We were nearing the corner when we passed a wide passageway leading back to a long irregular-shaped yard where there are a half-dozen five-story buildings. In front, facing the street, the houses are only three stories high.

The son of the Russian janitor, a clean, spectacled student, opens the door to one of the houses and shows us the apartments. There are three rooms, of fair size, all of them light and sunny on the top two floors. The living room has a fireplace and two many-paned windows facing south. The bedroom and kitchen face north and there is a window in each. There is a little toilet off the kitchen. Instead of a washtub, the boy says, the landlord will put in a bathtub. There is no heat, no hot water, no electricity, but the rent is only $10.00 a month.

The houses are sordid, grim, and look as though they belong in a Dickens novel. But Maria, who believes in scrubbing with strong yellow soap, is thinking of blue and white check curtains at the windows and her blue rag rugs on the floor.

"Blue, the psychologists say, is a happy color," she says cheerfully, not at all taken aback by the seven years' accumulation of dirt in the apartments, for it is long since they were occupied, the janitor's boy says.

"Blue is the color of the sky and the Blessed Virgin's robes."

"If we take the top floor, we can use the roof. There'll be plenty of blue then. Alan can build a fence to make it safe for the children."

Her mind is pretty well made up—Saint Joseph has helped us in our search, for really, the rooms envisaged with fresh paint, curtains, scrubbed floors, rag rugs and children's toys, are not so bad. A clear eye and a courageous spirit has transformed them into a home.

But it is too fine a day not to continue our walk, so we venture further into the depths of the East Side, down to Stanton Street to visit the model tenements of the Lavanburg Foundation. There had been stories in the paper a few weeks ago of the celebration of the fifth year of these model homes, built by the philanthropy, or shall we say, the loving kindness of a Jew, with the cooperation of his Catholic partner, two of whose sons are still on the board of trustees. Here there are roof gardens and basement club rooms, a kindergarten, and community activities. But the rents are $30.00 for three rooms, $34.00 for four rooms, and $42.00 for five rooms, low rents it is true, but too much for working people these days, when fathers of families are working half or full time for $10.00 and $15.00 a week and glad even of that to hold body and soul together.

"What should be done," said Maria, "is this. Landlords with the cooperativeness or sense of duty or whatever you want to call it, of Mr. Lavanburg, should take their old houses where the poor are still forced to live because they can't pay more than $10.00, $15.00 or $18.00 a month, and utilize the basements and roofs. There could be mothers' and fathers' clubs, and children's play clubs to meet in basement rooms for their activities. Community spirit and cooperation would be fostered. And the roofs could be made into playgrounds where they could gather together in summer instead of on crowded front stoops and garbage-filled streets, where the children are in continual danger. It wouldn't take much to make these reforms: only a landlord who has a social conscience and a few tenants who would cooperate and get things started. You don't have to have a million to do it. You don't have to have steam-heat and hot water. The poor are used to hardship. Small beginnings," she ruminated, as we walked back through dusky lamp-lit streets, for it was now five o'clock and twilight was upon us. "The roof playground first. . . . We'll see what we can do. . . ."

# Saint John of the Cross

# 13

---

"**W**E ARE POOR, but we are also rich," said Teresa sagely, in reference to a remark of the little girl upstairs whose mother had just bought a new kitchen stove. "As long as we have a roof over our heads and a few spoonfuls of food, we are rich."

"But I want more than a few spoonfuls of food," said Dickie, who was having dinner with us that night and who has a healthy twelve-year-old appetite. "I want two or three helpings."

So dishing out some more baked potatoes and string beans, I began to regale them with the poverty of Saint John of the Cross, whose life, by Father Bruno, I had been reading for the past week.

I told them about the hermitage of Calvario where Saint John lived for a time. The former prior there had been unbridled in his asceticism. The only food he allowed his hermits was raw herbs selected by Brother Alonso the cook, who led his mule along the mountainsides and looked at what it fed on so that he might collect it.

"A good many of them would have preferred that he should cease from troubling himself," the account written at the time reads.

On feast days they had a stew of breadcrumbs seasoned with oil, garlic and pepper, and so strict were the hermits that some criticized this relaxation as unnecessary.

"I would have eaten the mule," said Dickie stoutly buttering himself another slice of bread. "They ate horses during the war. I guess I coulda eaten mules."

Originally published in *Commonweal*, July 14, 1933. Vol. XVIII, 287–8.

"But Saint John wasn't so strict," I hastened to assure my guest. "He said that 'as men's minds are more inclined to society than to solitude, it was necessary in hermitages one should have a little more well-regulated corporeal solace than elsewhere,' so he must have remedied the scanty meals at Calvario, and then it could not have been so bad."

According to the account of Father Bruno who traveled all over Spain in the footsteps of Saint John, Calvario was a beautiful spot surrounded by orange, fig, almond and olive trees. The trouble with the place was that it was so small that the brothers were crowded and could not be alone. So at night John used to take them walking and after recreation by the banks of the stream which ran past the hermitage, he scattered his hermits to various points on the mountainside to make their evening meditation in peace and quiet."

"That is like us," said Teresa, spooning up her apple sauce. "Down in the country we have such a little, little house, it is like the colored people's houses down in Florida. So when we want to get away from people, we go walking on the beach and sing 'All ye works of the Lord.'"

"We never have enough room anywhere," said Dickie, who is a big fellow and finds it hard to dispose of his arms and legs. "If the rooms aren't too small, then there are always grandmothers and relatives hanging around and telling you to turn off the radio."

Saint Teresa, the good friend of Saint John, loved poverty dearly too. "The great honor of the poor is in being really poor," she says in her "Camino." But she adds that she made Saint Joseph her banker and never hesitated at any useful expenditure. "She was too supernatural and too intelligent to do things by halves," Father Bruno says. She herself writes, "Saint Teresa and three ducats is nothing, but God, Saint Teresa and three ducats is everything."

One of her first aims in her new houses was to see that her nuns had enough to eat, though she herself had to skimp often. One of the evils of the unreformed order lay in the fact that the convents were so poor (Reverend Father Rubeo after visiting them in 1567 forbade them to receive any more novices "for they would be in danger of dying of hunger") that the nuns fell into lax habits of sociability in order that they might receive from the hands of their friends sweetmeats and dainties to eat.

Saint Teresa not only loved poverty but she had a great respect for poor people, just as Saint John of the Cross had, and she was too "supernatural-minded" to turn away Andrada, the ragged young student at Toledo who offered to help the Sisters. "He had nothing but himself to help them with, he said," Saint Teresa writes in her "Foundations." "It amused me much and my companions more, to see what sort of assistance the holy man (Brother Martin of the Cross) had sent us; for his appearance was not that of a person for barefoot nuns to associate with."

But she asked him to find a house for them, which he did in a day. He told them it would be cleared out and for them to bring their things, and he expressed no surprise at the two mattresses and one blanket which Saint Teresa and her two companions had. "We went for some days with the mattresses and the blanket without more to cover us, and one day we had not even a bit of wood to broil a sardine," she writes. "At night we suffered a little from cold, for it was cold; however we covered ourselves with the blanket and with the serge cloaks which we wear over our habit, which have often been useful to us."

"She can't have been much more uncomfortable than I was all last winter," said Teresa's uncle, who is six feet and also young and gangling, "on that bed which folded up and had ridges in the middle and a mattress two inches thick. But I slept all right," he added.

I commended his saintly patience and continued my talk of the saints of those days. There were a great many of them—not only Saint Teresa and Saint John of the Cross. Father Bruno tells of Anne of Jesus, Beatrice of St. Michel, Catherine of St. Albert, Magdalene of the Holy Ghost, Frances of the Mother of God, Catherine of Jesus, Anne of Lobera and Marie de la Cruz. Catherine of the Conception, the holy Portuguese, was so gay "that she went to heaven laughing," as Saint Teresa put it.

They were all very gay and happy as a matter of fact. Blessed Anne of St. Bartholomew who knew Saint Teresa better than anyone, tells us "that she did not like melancholy people, that she herself was not gloomy and did not wish others to be so in her company; she used to say, 'May God deliver me from surly saints.'"

When Saint Teresa entered her convent to take the habit as a young girl, she went there dressed in an orange-colored dress with black velvet trimmings. She was always lighthearted—and I picked up Father Bruno's book to read some of it aloud.

"Teresa, like Saint Peter of Alcantara," he writes, "did not insist so much on mortifications of the flesh as on *desnudez*, the solitude and silence so necessary and fruitful for the spiritual life. . . . The primitive rule does not prescribe absolute silence, save from after Compline to Prime of the following day. Teresa, in order to put a stop to unnecessary conversation, settled on two hours of recreation, one in midday, the other in the evening, during which time 'things are so combined that we learn to know our own faults, at the same time enjoying relaxation which helps us the better to support the austerity of the rule. But the slightest detraction is strictly forbidden.' There is nothing cold or formal about these recreations she speaks of, which are so useful for acquiring self-knowledge. They have not the slightest appearance of prescribed duties. The Sisters chat as they work, for Teresa did not intend them to be idle. This does not prevent gaiety, even though there was no great desire for laughter. One day while she was still at Rio de Olmos, very tired and feverish, she was going to her cell at recreation time when a young lay Sister, a novice, who saw her slipping away, said to her: 'Are you not coming with us, Reverend Mother?' Teresa smiled and said, 'All right Sister, I'm coming.' She had a tabor and castanets, and she sang and danced. 'A queer sort of mother-foundress!'

"In her, the mystical impulse, poetry and childlike gaiety were all in harmony. She said to some peevish Sisters who took scandal, 'All this is needed to make life endurable.' Father John was not scandalized, and he acted in the same way more than once. He is a poet, the poet of the dark night, but also the poet of joy and love."

Before reading Father Bruno's book, I was acquainted with Saint John of the Cross only through the writings of Saint Teresa and through some translations of his poems. I knew very little about him, and though I was sure he was not a surly saint, I had thought him an extremely solitary one. So I was glad to find in Father Bruno's pages that his brother, Francisco de Yepes, was always his very dear friend and followed him in his wanderings often. And Catalina Alvarez, his mother, who had been left a widow early to support her two young sons by her silk weaving, came to his house at Duruelo from her home in Medina in order that she might cook for the Fathers in the first house of the reformed Carmelites. I thought as I read of the devoted Catalina, how Don Bosco's mother sold all that she had in order to help her son in his work for the youth of the city streets, and how she too came to live in his first house to help with the cooking and cleaning.

He was indeed poor, but, as little Teresa says, "he was also rich," this valiant saint!

# Houses of Hospitality                    14

I**N THE MIDDLE AGES** when one out of every four was leprous, there were two thousand leper houses run by religious in France alone. This is the startling and thought-provoking statement made in Farrow's book, "Damien, the Leper." That statement has not been contested. It may be horrifying to make such a comparison, but inasmuch as one out of every five workers today is unemployed or on work relief, the catastrophe which has visited us is comparable.

Unemployment is the gravest problem in the country today. It is immediate, so it is more pressing than the problem of war and peace. It means hunger and cold and sickness right now, so it is more immediate a problem than the unionizing of workers. In fact the unionizing of workers cannot get on while thirteen million men are unemployed and those employed are hanging on to their jobs like grim death and not willing to make any forward steps which would jeopardize those jobs. And we contend that the kind of shelter afforded these unattached unemployed is liable to make them leprous in soul and utterly incapable of working for sustenance or salvation.

There are thousands of men sheltered in the lodging houses of New York City, run by the city, and countless other thousands sitting up all night in missions and flop houses and roaming the streets. As the weather gets warmer you may see them sleeping in the shelter of

Originally published in *Commonweal*, April 15, 1938. Vol. XXVII, 683–4.

buildings, in areaways, in subways, along the waterfront. They crawl into their holes by night, and by day come out to tramp from one end of the island to the other in search of food. Every other city—Pittsburgh, Boston, Detroit, Chicago, Milwaukee, St. Louis—has the same problem.

Peter Maurin, whose idea it was to start the *Catholic Worker*, began it with a simple program which called for round-table discussions, houses of hospitality and farming communes. Before the depression, he predicted it. During the depression he constantly stressed the problem of unemployment. He is still journeying from one end of the country to the other, speaking of a new social order wherein man is human to man and which can be built up on the foundation of the works of mercy and voluntary poverty.

He himself has been a transient worker and an unemployed worker. He spent twenty years traveling through the United States and Canada, doing the manual labor which built this country. And it is due to his constant indoctrinating, as he calls it, that groups in New York, Boston, Pittsburgh, Chicago, Detroit, Milwaukee, Troy, St. Louis, Houma, Louisiana, and Windsor, Ontario, have started what Peter himself called from the beginning houses of hospitality, where those in need can receive food, clothing and shelter, and hold round table discussions, which point to the solution of problems. Peter is only doing what the great Saint Peter called for—working for a new heaven and a new earth, wherein justice dwelleth.

In New York, the unemployed come from all over, seeking work. They are not all single men. There are the married, as well as the sons of the family who leave home in order that they may not be a burden on those that remain. There are whole families migrating. There are young married couples. There are even lone women and girls.

Peter has always pointed out that according to canon law, all bishops should be running hospices, or houses of hospitality. But now, thinking in terms of state responsibility rather than personal responsibility, those in need are turned over to agencies, to the city or the state. There are isolated instances of hospices of the homeless of course. I have visited Father Dempsey's huge hospice in St. Louis, for instance. Father Dempsey was criticized for "bringing all the bums in the United States to St. Louis." But nevertheless his work was well supported and he was able to carry on his work for many, many years. There is a splendid hospice run by the St. Vincent de Paul Society in San Francisco, where a small charge of $.15 is made. There is a day shelter besides where men can remain during inclement weather. We believe of course that an absolutely free place is necessary for the wanderer not having any funds or not knowing the ropes. I have heard of a hospice in Philadelphia which I wish to visit, and doubtless there are many more. I hope readers of this article will let me know of others throughout the country, run under Catholic auspices.

I have visited all the hospices run by *Catholic Worker* groups, naturally, and they all have the same difficulties and the same problems and are all run on the same lines. They all started with no funds at all. A small group got together, decided they wanted a headquarters for propaganda and meetings, and rented a store for $10 or $15 a month. None of them ever knew where the next month's rent was coming from. Usually there was no money for paint or soap or mops or beds or stoves or cups. But little by little these things were contributed. Most of them began fearfully and are continuing fearfully. If any of them ever thought they were going to have to feed the numbers they are feeding, they would never have had the courage to start. (Oh, we of little faith!) Most of them hesitated along for several years before starting the endless task of feeding those who came. For as soon as the feeding began —as soon as the mood of hospitality began to make itself felt—lines formed at the door, and continued day after day.

In New York, our breakfast line, which began with a single friendly pot of coffee on the stove in the store where we hold our meetings, grew and grew until now we serve breakfast to approximately 1,000 men. They begin forming on the line at four-thirty in the morning. The door is not opened until six and then the work goes on until nine or nine-thirty. During the day we have only sixty or so to the other two meals. We have to consider the work of the paper, letter writing, receiving visitors, taking care of those under our roof which number about fifty in the city and fifteen in the country. (In the summer there will be about fifty there too.)

In Boston they feed 250 men a day; in Pittsburgh 200; in Detroit, 400; St. Louis, 200; and so on. The numbers are not so large, but if the reader will just contemplate saying to himself, "Two or three friends and I will undertake to feed 350 people a meal every day," not just for one day but indefinitely, stretching out month after month, year after year, he would be aghast. Just try it. He would not think it possible by himself of course, nor would he trust the Lord to fall in with his seemingly presumptuous plans.

Yet if we are thinking in terms of personal responsibility, to those who sit around and say, "Why don't the priests do this or that?" or

"Why don't *they* [that indefinite *they*] do this or that?" we should reply, "Why don't *we all?*"

It is really the work of the lay apostolate. In this day of huge parishes, running into thousands of souls (sometimes even 10,000) it is hard to see how the priest can think of undertaking such a work. Bishops used to have personal knowledge and acquaintance with not only all their priests but many of their flock, whereas now the bishop of a large diocese has every moment taken with spiritual duties.

We not only believe that this is the work of the lay apostolate, but we believe that all over the country the faithful should gird up their loins, so to speak, and start two thousand houses. If France could start and continue for a few generations two thousand leper houses, until segregation, combined with the plague, wiped out leprosy, then surely we in the United States ought to be able to open and continue two thousand houses of hospitality and face the prospect of continuing them not only through this generation but until the social order has been reconstructed.

It is a grave emergency. The Holy Father says that the workers of the world are being lost to the Church. If we are all lay apostles and "other Christs" this is our responsibility.

Trade union leaders like John L. Lewis believe that through strong unions, labor leaders in politics, legislation, the thirty-hour week, insurance, taxation, and public works financed through taxation of industrialists rather than of the poor through sales taxes, the unemployed can be reabsorbed and those not reabsorbed can be taken care of.

Perhaps a Christian state could do all these things. But since we are living under only a nominally Christian state, Christians will have to resort to those old-as-the-Church itself methods of the works of mercy through houses of hospitality to care for immediate needs such as food, clothing and shelter.

These needs supplied under Christian auspices would make a startling change in the character of the unemployed. Hope, that most sinned-against of virtues would be restored. Hospices in the shadow of churches would mean a constant recognition of Christ the Worker, Christ our Brother. The priests living in close contact with the poorest of transients and ministering to them, holy Mass, missions, constant indoctrination through Catholic literature, Catholic surroundings— what a change this would make in the outlook of the poor!

As it is now, under the dubious hospitality of the city and state, it is as though God were unknown. There is no reminder to morning and evening prayer. Men have lost the sense of their own dignity, that dignity which they possess because Christ shared their humanity, their unemployment, their dire need.

Worse than that, men become drunken, drug-ridden, vicious and obscene in many cases. These are strong words but when one thinks what mobs are capable of, once their passions are aroused, it must be admitted that in our care for the poor we do nothing to give man the power to control his baser nature which through its black deeds most assuredly merits the hell which Christ died to save us from.

Who are most prominent in caring for transients and unemployed throughout the country? The Workers Alliance with its millions of members is strictly Marxist and materialist in its philosophy, however unformulated. There amongst those masses is the material for revolutionary mobs, and when we consider revolutions in the past, engineered by the few intellectual leaders with a theory of revolution as Lenin called it, when we consider the mass riots in New York in the last century which led to the building of our many armories, we can count on a well-directed mob throughout the country under the influence of whatever Marxist leaders or Fascist leaders that turn up in the future.

Unless—.

# The House on Mott Street                              15

---

IN VIEW OF THE FACT that all workers in the New York house of hospitality live on Mott Street instead of in scattered homes as they do in our other centers where there are only one or two in charge, it may seem that there are many to do the work in New York. But our staff is not so large. Peter Maurin and I are traveling and speaking a great deal, and I have a large correspondence and much writing to do besides the monthly paper to edit. William Callahan has been managing editor for the past two years, but he also has to travel and speak, besides handling details of management. Edward Priest has been forced to live away from the work the past year and a half and can give little time to it. John Curran handles correspondence and travels; Ade Bethune lives in Newport and works there. Other members of the staff whose names do not appear on the masthead are similarly occupied. John Cort has his time taken up completely by the Association of Catholic Trade Unionists; Tim O'Brien by the Catholic Union of Unemployed; Pat Whalen and Martin Flynn help John Cort; which leaves at present only Joe Zarella in the office with Julia Porcell giving her afternoons. Cy Echele and Herb Welch help with the coffee line in the morning, which means four hours' work, and then sell papers on the streets all afternoon. This street apostolate is of great importance. Other members of the group are on the farming commune.

Originally published in *Commonweal,* May 6, 1938. Vol. XXVIII, 37–9.

The young men take turns on the line every morning so that usually each one is called upon just two mornings a week. (It is an interesting fact that these works of mercy are carried on by young men throughout the country. Young women are either occupied with their families or prospective families so that other aid must come from them. Then, too, much of our work, dealing in general with masses of men, is unsuitable for women.)

New York has more than its share of visitors so we have many guests who are interested in the work and in the social ideas of Peter Maurin. Often we have visitors from early morning until late at night, coming to every meal and remaining for discussions which go on at all times of the day, when two or three are gathered together. (I recall one such discussion when last summer three young priests met for the first time at the *Catholic Worker*—one from California, one from Texas and one from New York—and have been fast friends ever since. They spent the entire afternoon with us and stayed to supper.)

Because of the crowds of callers and visitors for one or two weeks' stay, it is harder to get all the work done sometimes than if we had just two or three running the place. More people means more work, as every woman knows. The fewer there are, the less there is to do. The fewer there are running one particular work, the more gets done very often. Witness a clumsy committee of thirty as compared to a committee of three.

Other groups contemplating starting a house of hospitality will argue, "You have the paper to help support the work." Yet experience has shown that the work gets support wherever it is started, and the support continues. Some fear that they will withdraw local support from the New York group and the paper. And yet, in spite of flourishing houses in the big cities of Boston, Pittsburgh, Detroit, Chicago, Milwaukee and St. Louis, they keep going and so do we.

It is true that it is never easy. God seems to wish us to remain poor and in debt and never knowing where we are going to get the money to pay our grocery bills or provide the next meal. While writing this, we have nothing in the bank and are sending out an appeal for help this month.

But we are convinced that this is how the work should go. We are literally sharing the poverty of those we help. They know we have nothing, so they do not expect much and they even try to help. Some of our best workers have been recruited from the unemployed line. They are not going to a magnificent building to get meager aid. They are not going to contemplate with bitterness the expensive buildings to be kept up, and perhaps paid for on the installment plan, and compare it with their state. They are not going to conjecture as to the property and holdings of the Church and criticize how their benefactors live while they suffer destitution.

The trouble is, in America, Catholics are all trying to keep up with the other fellow, to show, as Peter Maurin puts it, "I am just as good as you are," when what they should say is, "I am just as bad as you are."

There are no hospices because people want to put up buildings which resemble the million-dollar Y.M.C.A.s. If they can't do it right they won't do it at all. There is the Italian proverb, "The best is the enemy of the good." Don Bosco had a good companion who was always not wanting to do things because they could not be done right. But he went right ahead and took care of his boys in one abandoned building after another, being evicted, threatened with an insane asylum and generally looked upon as a fool. Rose Hawthorne who founded the cancer hospital at Hawthorne, New York, started in a small apartment in an east side tenement, not waiting for large funds to help her in the work.

Once the work of starting houses of hospitality is begun, support comes. The Little Flower has shown us her tremendous lesson of "the little way." We need that lesson especially in America where we want to do things in a big way or not at all.

A small store is sufficient to start the work. One pot of soup or a pot of coffee and some bread is sufficient to make a beginning. You can feed the immediate ones who come and God will send what is needed to continue the work. He has done so over and over again in history. We often think of the widow's cruse when we contemplate our coffee pots. When the seamen during the 1936–1937 strike asked us where we got the wherewithal to feed the fifteen hundred of them a day who wandered in for three months, we reminded them of the loaves and fishes. And they had faith in our goodwill, and in our poverty too, for many of them took up collections on their ships after the strike was over to try to repay us. We have four seamen still with us, two of them joining the movement with their whole hearts and contributing everything they have to it. One came back from a trip and gave us all he had, $160.

What is really necessary, of course, and it is not easy, is that one put everything he has into the work. It is not easy to contemplate, of course, but for those who feel called to do the work, if they honestly give everything they have, God takes care of the work abundantly. We have to remember the case of Ananias who was trying to hold out, even while he wished to enjoy the privileges of belonging to the group.

This sounds extreme, but since Father Paul Hanley Furfey published his book, "Catholic Extremism," people have not been so afraid of the word or of the idea. Father Furfey has played an important part in clarifying ideas, building up a theory of revolution. Lenin said, "There can be no revolution without a theory of revolution," and that holds good for the Catholic revolution.

"The little way," faith in God and the realization that it is He that performs the work, and lastly, not being afraid of dirt and failure, and criticism. These are the things which must be stressed in holding up the technique of works of mercy as a means of regaining the workers to Christ.

We have read so many advertisements about germs and cleanliness and we think so much of modern improvements, plumbing, prophylaxis, sterilization, that we need to read again, thinking in terms of ourselves, what our Lord said to His Apostles: "Not what goeth into a man, but what proceedeth from a man defileth him."

Please understand that we are not averse to the progress of science. We think of cleanliness with longing and never hope to achieve it. We spend money on food instead of on fresh paint and I defy anyone to make an old tenement clean with plain scrubbing. Antique plumbing, which goes with poverty and tenements, cold water, no baths, worn wood full of splinters that get under the nails, stained and chipped baseboards, tin ceilings, all these things, besides the multitudes that come in and out every day, make for a place that gets pretty dirty. And we get plenty of criticism for it, the justice and injustice of which must be acknowledged. Sometimes it rains or snows and then two thousand feet tracking in the muck from the street makes the place hopeless. But if we waited until we had a clean place before we started to feed and house people, we'd be waiting a long time and many would go hungry.

Peter has always stressed the value of manual labor, and that the worker should be a scholar and the scholar a worker. He also firmly believes that those who are considered leaders must be servants. Christ washed the feet of His disciples.

So in the history of the *Catholic Worker*, we have all done a good deal of cooking, dishwashing, scrubbing of toilets and halls, cleaning of beds, washing of clothes, and in a few cases even of washing human beings. (Once Peter and I were scrubbing the office over on 15th Street, he starting at the front and I in the back. And Peter, believing as he does in discussion, paused again and again to squat on his haunches while he discoursed, I having to stop in order to hear him. It took us all day! He is a better scrubber than he is a dishwasher. You have to put all your attention on greasy dishes when you heat all the water to wash up after sixty people. Another time I was washing baby clothes for one of the girls in the house of hospitality and Peter joined in the rinsing of them. Now there are so many of us on Mott Street that there is a distribution of toil, and a worker is liable to take offense if his job is taken away from him even for a day, regarding it as a tacit form of criticism. But on the farm there is always plenty of opportunity for the most menial tasks.)

Also, most important of all, one must not be surprised at criticism. We all find it hard to take, and one good thing about it is that it shows us constantly how much pride and self-love we have. But take it we must, and not allow ourselves to be discouraged by it. It is never going to be easy to take, and it is a lifetime job to still the motions of wrath on hearing it. Criticisms such as these:

"What good does it all do anyway? You don't do anything but feed them. They need to be rehabilitated. You might better take fewer responsibilities and do them well. You have no right to run into debt. . . ."

In regard to the debt, all of us at the *Catholic Worker* consider ourselves responsible for the debts we contract. If our friends did not come to our assistance, if we did not make enough by writing and speaking and by publishing the paper to pay them, and if therefore we were forced to go "out of business" as the saying is, we would all get jobs as dishwashers or houseworkers if necessary and pay off our debts to the last farthing. And our creditors know this and trust us. At that, we have fewer debts than most papers, considering the coffee line and the number of people we are supporting.

All criticisms are not reasonable. One woman writes in to tell us we must get separate drinking cups for all the men. A man writes to tell us to serve oatmeal and a drink made of roasted grains and no bread. For a thousand people! And the latest criticism is the following, written on a penny postal and not signed. It is the second of its kind during the week.

"Out of curiosity I stopped at your bread line today. I saw several men making (as they term it) the line two or three times, actually eating the bread in the line. This is the schedule of a number of the men in whom you are interested: 1st trip, South Ferry, breakfast; 2nd trip, morning, 115 Mott Street; 3rd trip, morning, St. Francis, West 31st Street. I heard Jack tell Tom he must go right then to Water Street, be there not later than 11:45 so as to be in time for South Ferry at one o'clock. The writer ventures to say that 95 percent of your men are not worth powder to shoot them."

God help these poor men, traveling from place to place, wandering the streets, in search of food. Bread and coffee here, bread and oatmeal there, a sandwich some place else, and a plate of stew around noon. Never a meal. Many of them lame and halt and unable to travel, and living on a sandwich and a cup of coffee from morning to night.

There is not much time to think of one's soul when the body cries out for food. "You cannot preach the gospel to men with empty stomachs," Abbé Lugan says.

So we make our plea for houses of hospitality which in the shadow of the church recall men to Christ and to the job of rebuilding the social order. Catholic France had 2,000 leper houses during that time of emergency in the Middle Ages. We are confronted by an emergency today, a need that only Christians can supply. We must bring workers to Christ as it has been done down through the ages and is being done today in all missionary lands.

I quote the Holy Father on works of mercy:

"The preaching of truth did not make many conquests for Christ. The preaching of truth led Christ to the cross. It is through charity that He has gained souls and brought them to follow Him. There is no other way for us to gain them. Look at the missionaries. Through which way do they convert the pagans? Through the good deeds which they multiply about them. You will convert those who are seduced by communist doctrines in the measure you will show them that the faith in Christ and the love of Christ are inspired by personal interest and good deeds. You will do it in the measure that you will show them that nowhere else can be found such a source of charity."

# Tale of Two Capitals 16

1939 sees no end to human misery in the United States. Here are reports from Washington and Harrisburg.

### Washington

IT IS A HOT SUMMER AFTERNOON in Washington, but there is a good breeze coming in the windows as I write. The radio is going in the front room—soothing waltzes—and Mary is sitting in a flowered voile dress embroidering a doily. Mary is quite black and her dress is very fresh and white, and she is a picture, cool and calm. She has set the two big tables for supper, which is her share of the evening's work. She and her two sisters have also helped me to peel potatoes in the back yard. The beans have been strung and Miss Selew has seared the meat and it is now simmering away in a deep pan, covered with good brown gravy. Betty Walsh soon comes in from her classes at the Catholic University to finish up the job and serve. It is her turn, but she has been giving an examination, so everyone had jumped into the breach.

Dinner is served at Il Poverello House on Tenth Street in Washington every night at six-thirty, and swarms of the children of the neighborhood come in. There are three little girls living in the house and two big girls, both graduates of Francis Xavier University in New Orleans, now finishing up a year of graduate work at the Catholic University. These,

Originally published in *Commonweal*, July 14, 1939. Vol. XXX, 288–90.

with the two older women, who teach at the University, make up the family.

But everyone in the neighborhood considers the house a sort of headquarters and comes for aid of one kind or another. The doors are open when the women get home from school and the work of hospitality goes on. Bedtime is early, because everyone gets up at quarter past five to offer the Mass at the shrine at quarter of six, where they all make the responses together, and where Father Paul Hanley Furfey gives a short homily every day. It's a good way of starting the day, and the early morning is cool and fragrant as we drive over to the shrine.

The life of the group at Il Poverello house is dedicated to voluntary poverty. The principle is, "If we have less, everyone will have more." So on this very immediate practical idea, many are helped.

They certainly need help, the Negroes in Washington. Down the alley in back of this house—it is a two-story, box-like structure for which the rent is $75 a month—the tiny little houses with no running water, rent for $16 a month. Quite literally they are hovels. Places that would rent for $8 a month in New York cost twice as much here. And places are hard to find.

Washington is a beautiful city; the streets are tree-shaded and on the streets the houses are mostly not bad. But down the alleys live the great mass of poor, crowded in dirty, evil-smelling, little holes. There the unemployed hang out, dull and lethargic, some vicious and dissipated, as well as the greater number who struggle against terrific odds to keep themselves human, to rise above their surroundings.

### The Blessed Martin Home

Down at 1215 Seventh Street, Llewellyn Scott manages his house of hospitality which he calls the Blessed Martin Home. The address is on Seventh Street but the entrance is down the alley. On the door hangs a crucifix. The stairs leading to the two floors above a barber shop are dark and rickety. On the walls are holy pictures and in the two sitting rooms upstairs are many more. There are beds everywhere, even in the front living room, which is filled with books and some easy chairs. In this room a very old man sleeps.

"I don't like to put him in with the others; they get to talking and arguing and make him nervous," Llewellyn said. "The other night two of them in the other sitting room were arguing about what they had been able to see out of their jail windows at Leavenworth and they were getting wild. I had to go in and shush them. I never have any trouble and nobody ever gets rough. In the three years I've been running the place, we've never had the police in."

Llewellyn Scott is a colored man who works part time for the government. Out of his salary he supports an aged mother and an invalid sister: pays their rent, which is partly covered by two roomers, and feeds them. He uses the rest of his meager resources to keep the Blessed Martin House going. During the past year he has served 17,780 meals and during the winter he put up about forty-five men a night. Today there were fifteen men sleeping in the house, as many as the beds could hold.

The place is terribly dilapidated. Paper hangs from the walls, and underneath the plaster has fallen off and the slats show. The floor slopes in every direction and you walk up and down a grade as you go from room to room. The rent is $26 a month. It is unheated, and in winter they can afford only two gallons of oil a day to try to keep it warm. Down on the first floor in what was originally a big storeroom, he has made a chapel and lined it with corrugated cardboard. There an altar is set up with a statue of the Sacred Heart. Today there were flowers in front of it, peonies and dahlias. They had spent twenty-five cents which a woman had given them (they had been praying for her sick daughter)—money which they might have spent for food. There are plenty of chairs in the chapel and four *prie-dieux*. Here at five-thirty every night they gather for the rosary and the litany. Most of the men who come to the place are not Catholics, but they soon learn the prayers and they all love to sing.

"The Board of Health came and made me take out some of the beds," Llewellyn said. "They wanted to know if I had a covered garbage can. I told them garbage cans were for rich folks. We have nothing to throw away. When we have nothing we don't eat. But down the street a Jewish baker gives us bread."

John J. O'Brien, veteran, sat with us there as we talked. On the window sill a tiny black kitten washed itself with a bright pink tongue. John had just hiked down from Chester, Pennsylvania. He had been in Philadelphia, visiting the Catholic Worker house there, and he talked of the conditions in Chester. Fifteen hundred men just thrown out of work by a factory which was moving south, and a few hundred men just let off a ship. We ought to start a place there.

John started a place here in Washington recently but it only lasted two months. He started with too much rent, $45 a month, which he paid out of money he had saved from his small pension. He had visited the place in Pittsburgh and it was there he got the idea. Houses of hospitality for men all over the country. Using all the unoccupied buildings. The men building up self-help groups, working together for mutual aid.

His place didn't last because John became terrified. Convents and monasteries started sending him their mendicants and he was not able to handle them all. He didn't know how to feed them, how to live from day to day. He didn't know that Saint Joseph is supposed to handle those things for us. He had expected that human agencies would step in and help once the thing got started, and when no one came to help he got discouraged.

Last month the house closed up and he passed on the furniture to Llewellyn. Now, however, he is determined to start again, this time with a smaller place and expecting nothing. "I'll do what I can myself, and I'm not going to stop. I'm going to keep after this. I'll start now the little way."

It's a strange fight for the weather-bitten veteran, clad in dungarees, used to the roads and the men who are tramping the roads. It's a new kind of a fight, but something has to be done.

"We'll do what we can," he repeated, "and some day they'll take these unoccupied buildings and start some hospices. A place to live and something to eat now, and then we can plan on what to do. Then we can plan on getting back the land."

## Harrisburg

All the Catholic Worker houses of hospitality aim to be poor. They are in the slums but somehow we never get down quite low enough. There are always a few rungs lower to go on the ladder of destitution. Besides when we get through scrubbing and painting or whitewashing, there is a decent look about the houses which contrasts greatly with other places in the neighborhood. Llewellyn Scott's place in Washington is poverty stricken and dilapidated beyond hope of repair. The building just won't stand it. The house in Philadelphia has an outside toilet, a shanty in back, but, unlike other places in the neighborhood, at least it is not one to be shared with five other houses.

Here is Harrisburg there just isn't any toilet. You go next door to the neighbors. And there was no running water until a week ago. Most of the houses on the block have no running water. The neighbors pay one man down the street for the privilege of getting pails of water from his house.

Our place, the Blessed Martin Home, is two rooms, now scrubbed clean. There is electricity, tables and chairs, magazines to read. There is paint and linoleum on the floor, the linoleum donated out of her salary by a colored cook who works all day and then comes over to help us in the evening.

There is a faucet in the kitchen now, but no sink. We are begging for that.

The women, colored and white, who are engaging in the Catholic Worker activities among the children and families in the neighborhood, are supporting themselves and there is little money to spare. They have to advance little by little, at a snail's pace.

Due to lack of decent living facilities, no one is resident in the house permanently, but different families have been given the use of the place as a temporary lodging—two white families with thirteen and seven children respectively and one colored family with seven children.

How they got along in two rooms with no water and no toilet is hard to understand. But these families had been evicted in the quiet, orderly way Harrisburg, capital of Pennsylvania, has of doing such things. A moving van drives up to the door, the furniture is carted out and put in storage. The family is turned into the streets to roam around until some welfare agency or relief bureau takes the case up and resettles them. Then they pay for moving into their next place. In one case the children were rolled out of bed and left in their night things as the clothes and bedding were loaded on the van. Even the ice box with some food in it was taken. Neighbors sheltered the evicted family.

Our house sheltered Lucille, too. Lucille was a colored girl, twenty-three years old. She was found dying in an empty house by Mary Frecon, who is our Harrisburg representative. Lucille grew up on the streets. She and her brothers and sisters just prowled around, living as best they could. For the last few months, ravaged with syphilis and drink, Lucille had been cared for by an old colored man who lived in an abandoned shed down an alley. He gave her his cot—that and a chair were the only things he had—and he waited on her as best he could. But the flies were eating her alive, huge horse flies, and in her agony she crawled out and sought shade and relief in an abandoned house next to ours where another old colored man had taken refuge. He too took care of her—they know the uselessness of appealing to agencies—until the neighbors told Mary about it. She found her moaning and crying and trying to beat away the flies that fastened themselves on her open sores.

The few women who carry on the Catholic Worker activities here brought her into their clean little rooms and there they tried to take care of her.

Not a hospital in Harrisburg would have her and it was only after five days that Dr. Boland got an ambulance from Steelton (they could not get one at Harrisburg) and sent her to the House of the Good Shepherd at Philadelphia where they deposited her without a word and with no papers about her case. The House of the Good Shepherd is not a hospital, but it is for such girls as Lucille had been. So they took her in, nursed her, and there she died not many weeks later.

While she was lying over in the Catholic Worker house she had been baptized and anointed by Father Kirchner of St. Patrick's Cathedral.

Harrisburg is full of Lucilles and a few visits to the slums there can explain why.

After we visited the children and some of the neighbors at 1019 Seventh Street tonight, we went across the street to Mrs. Wright. She lives in a rickety two-storied house, owned by the city and completely out of repair. The banisters are falling down and the steps are unsafe. Here in the only two habitable rooms, she, her seven children, her husband and another woman have refuge. They have three beds and they all sleep in one room. The kitchen is only big enough for the stove, the table and a few chairs.

Mrs. Wright sat there with her youngest baby, six months old, on her lap. He is thin and moans constantly. He has had pneumonia and whooping cough, one house burned down around him and the other day the whole ceiling came down upon his crib. He has lived through these six months, but from the look of him he will not live much longer, poor baby. And God knows he will be happier dead. It is hard to see the look of settled sadness on the faces of the others.

Mary Frecon and Jean Records tried to clean the place up for them. They went in with pails and mops and with cold water and plenty of soap they scrubbed and scoured. But it didn't show. The hot foul air caught at our throats as we went in, and half strangled us.

Mary Frecon, married and with a family to look after, is not able to live in the house of hospitality at Harrisburg, but she has certainly made her home another CW unit. Right now she has a young woman with two small babies, one and three years old, living with her. She picked them up at one of the evictions she was covering. The girl's husband has abandoned her and she has endured great hardships. There were even nights before her second baby was born that she sat out on doorsteps all night. For the last year or so she had been making her home with other poor families and working for them.

The greatest difficulty in Harrisburg is to find a home to live in, even when a family is on relief and has money to pay rent. Housing seems to be the greatest immediate problem of the city. But thanks to Mary Frecon and the Harrisburg Housing Association which she has built up (it is an interracial group) there is now $1,800,000 available for housing projects and half of it is going for the Negro. Not much, but something to start on. Mary is interested in projects which will enable the residents to have land where they can raise their own food, but it will take a great fight to put that over. But she is a fighter, and we are hoping that her efforts will see to it that this new housing is for the truly poor and not just for middle-class salaried workers, as it usually is.

# Letter:
# In the Name of the Staff

# 17

IN THE NAME OF the staff of *The Catholic Worker,* Peter Maurin, Adé Béthune, William Callahan, Joe Zarella, Gerald Griffin and Edward Priest, I write to assure you of our prayers on your fifteenth anniversary. We are grateful to you for all the pioneering work you have done in the past, and for all the help the editors personally and through their columns have given us.

You remember that Peter Maurin always says that it is the duty of the journalist to make history as well as record it. May THE COMMONWEAL continue to have the influence on its times that it has had in the past.

Originally published in *Commonweal,* November 3, 1939. Vol. XXXI, 59.

# King, Ramsay and Connor 18

The story of three men convicted of a murder of which they knew nothing.

W E DROVE OVER Golden Gate Bridge through the warm spring sunshine, and for half an hour through the mountains over a four lane highway. Dick Bourret of the Young Christian Workers was driving, and Miriam Tinkin of the Defense Committee and a girl from the American Writers League had come along. We talked about the case as we drove, and we were not paying much attention to the scene about us.

The Defense Committee is supported by the California State Federation of Labor, by the Maritime Federation of the Pacific, by the Alameda and San Pedro, Portland and Seattle Central Labor Councils.

The three men we were going to see were members of the Marine Firemen division of the Maritime Federation and were convicted in Oakland, California, of a crime of which they knew nothing, the murder of an engineer on the *Point Lobos* in March, 1936.

The *Point Lobos,* a freighter, was docked in Alameda, across the bay from San Francisco. On that morning two men saw a seaman by the name of Wallace and identified him later at the trial. One testified that Wallace had asked him to go over to the *Point Lobos* with him in order to get this engineer. Another, the second engineer on the *Point Lobos,*

Originally published in *Commonweal,* April 19, 1940. Vol. XXXI, 551–2.

testified that he saw Wallace coming out of the cabin of the engineer who was murdered, George Alberts.

When the arrests were made in August, just before the beginning of the 1936–37 strike, not only Wallace was arrested, but Earl King, head of the firemen, San Francisco vice-president of the Martime Federation; Earnest Ramsay, patrolman for the firemen; and Connor, ship's delegate on the *Point Lobos.*

King is today a man of 46, Connor 44, Ramsay 30, after having served three years. For, unbelievable as it may seem after reading the testimony, the three men, together with Wallace, were convicted.

The contention of the prosecution is that King hired Ramsay to beat up Alberts, and that Connor, Wallace, a seaman called Sakovitz, who is supposed to have dealt with death blow, were the ones responsible for the murder. But even the prosecution proved that King and Ramsay were in San Francisco at the time. Connor was on duty in the engine room of the ship at the time. Sakovitz never has been found.

For the whole involved story, it is best to get the pamphlets issued, one entitled "The Ship Murder," the other, "Punishment without Crime," both obtainable from the Maritime Federation of the Pacific, 24 California Street, San Francisco. Both pamphlets cost a nickel. Knowing how responsive the readers of *Commonweal* are to the cry for justice, I confidently urge them to get the pamphlets and write to Governor Olson their opinion in regard to the case. They will thus be performing many of the works of mercy.

### Visiting the men

The business of this article is to tell of my visit with the men at San Quentin. They had read *The Catholic Worker* for the past two years, so they knew the paper, and we plunged right into conversation.

"I've been studying carpentry while I'm here," King said, "so that if I ever go back to the land I'll be able to build me chicken houses."

I've heard that many a time from seamen. When at sea they dream of the land, it is always of the farm, not of the city.

None of the men are Catholic, though Connor was baptized a Catholic back in Boston. He did not go to parochial schools, he said. King is a Presbyterian. Needless to say, none of the men are churchgoers.

"I might have gone yesterday, Easter Sunday," Connor said, "but the place was too crowded." There is one priest, Father O'Meara, for all the Catholics in San Quentin.

You look at the pictures of the three men as they appear on the cover of one of the pamphlets, and then look at them as they are today, and you see the tragic mark of prison life. King, a huge fellow with a chest like a barrel, has grown stout with the inactivities of prison life. All the work he has to do is sweeping his cell block. There are twice as many men there as the prison is supposed to hold, so naturally there is not enough work for them all. There are two in a cell, and Ramsay complained that his reading was interrupted. He liked travel books and biographies, and he never got through more than a few pages without the man in the lower bunk calling up, "Say, Red!" (Ramsay has curly red hair.)

All three of them do a lot of reading, books their friends send them, such as "Factories in the Fields," "Grapes of Wrath," newspapers and magazines. None of them subscribe to the prison library; they say the books are not much good and they are dirty, pages missing, and it's too much trouble. But their friends have kept them supplied.

The grub is good, and they described the Easter dinner. A year ago there were food riots at San Quentin and forty of the prisoners were badly beaten by the guards.

Outside the big room where we sat at a counter facing the men, the scene was bright; there was the prospect of rolling hills. As we drove in, we passed a line of prisoners working on one hillside, among them one of the strikers from the Salinas Lettuce strike who had assaulted a scab. He had not been badly injured, but the striker got ten years.

There are wide flower gardens around the place, there are the quiet waters of the bay reaching up to the very gates of the prison, there is freedom, light and joy, outside those windows, and one's heart is constricted facing three men held behind bars.

While there are men in prison, we are not free, Debs had said.

As long as the members suffer, the health of the whole body is lowered, and these men are members of the Mystical Body of Christ. They are our brothers, sons of the same Father.

Connor is suffering the most because he, after a third degree grilling, signed a confession which he immediately repudiated from his hospital bed where he had to be taken after his three-day ordeal. It takes every effort on the part of the others to keep his courage up. It eats into him continually. He broods over it, he is sensitive on the subject, he is overcome with a sense of guilt which the loyalty and friendship of the others does not seem to be able to disperse. He needs our prayers. King suffers, but is matter of fact. "As long as a man keeps his self respect, he can stand anything," he says. When he gets out, he will go on with his union work; there is a job before him.

Ramsay admits a man can never be the same again. It does something to him; if he didn't have the union in back of him he'd go nuts. "You see them cracking up around here all the time."

What makes it worse is that the men, although they have been found guilty in the court of second degree murder which carries with it a sentence of from five years to life, have not actually had the terms of their imprisonment set. As I write, they expect to be sentenced, and after they are sentenced, their cases can come before the pardon board, not before. The ruling is that the sentence must be set when they have served half of the minimum, but they have passed that by eight months. They live in constant expectation, in hope that is continually disappointed. They wait, they expect, they hear nothing and they steel themselves to wait some more.

### Our talk

We talked for the full hour we were permitted, sometimes to one man, and sometimes the conversation was general. King spoke most on the story of the union struggle in San Francisco, the struggle for leadership in the unions, the planting of company men among the union leaders, the need for education of the rank and file.

We talked of books, of the war, of the prospect of freedom. The time passed quickly. The visit seemed very brief, but even after that short hour, one would not be able to forget the faces of the men, their grim endurance, their haggard anxiety as we spoke of the possibilities of some action on the part of the parole board. I can see them now as I write; they are men one cannot forget.

In the afternoon after my visit to San Quentin, I was walking along Sutter Street in San Francisco. There were flower stalls on the corners. The air was filled with fragrance. In one of the department stores there was a display of Walt Disney cartoons for "Pinocchio." I stopped to look at it, I window-shopped at other stores. I was free, I could choose what I wished to do, where I would eat, whom I would see, where I would go. And tears came to my eyes. I was free, but not those men out at San Quentin, not many another weary prisoner. Along Market Street the crowds are sauntering all the day, seamen off their ships are sauntering, debating how they will spend their free time. But not those men at San Quentin. The sunlight is a mockery to them.

But we can do something.

We can help them bear their burden. We can help them by remembering them in our prayers.

Back at Mott Street at the house of hospitality there is hanging on the wall of my room a painting by van Gogh, of prison walls, and a circle of prisoners. It is there to remind me to pray for the prisoners.

We can help by sending for the pamphlets which tell the details of the case against these men. We can help by writing to Governor Olsen of California.

And as I write this, I write it fearfully, because it is putting a great responsibility on you who read. If you hear of this, just one of the cases of injustice in our industrial civilization, and you turn aside and do nothing, you are like the man who left his neighbor wounded on the roadside. "If you did not know, you would not have sin." But now, knowing, you must do something. And I know you will.

# It Was a Good Dinner     19

Summer in the city is hard, particularly in poor neighbor-hoods.

I N SUMMER it is hard. Everybody goes away on vacations and those who can't go away are sending others away. Students have finished paying expenses for one year and are looking forward to paying expenses for another year at school. Nobody has any money, especially those who want to help, who are the most generous.

I don't know how we could make out if it were not for the free vegetables we are getting this summer. Free rolls and cakes too. We go on charging our coffee, sugar and milk, and a great supply of bread, 250 pounds a day. And of course we have to buy meat. Once in a while we can get a supply of fish from the Fulton Market, a barrelful at a time, and then the cleaning takes place in the backyard, and if it is fish with roe in it we fry up the roe and there is an afternoon tea party with fish-roe sandwiches, everybody prowling around like cats, licking their chops.

It is fun cleaning the fish in the courtyard between the houses. A long table is brought out and everybody who can find a knife joins in. We have to cook the entire barrelful and everyone has to eat as much as he can. It would be dangerous to keep it, as our icebox never seems to get very cold. The difficulty is to get fat to fry the fish. It takes a lot of lard to fry a barrelful. But oh, the smell while it is cooking! It is enough to reconcile one to the other smells which hang over the backyard for a few days after.

Originally published in *Commonweal*, August 23, 1940. Vol. XXXII, 364–5.

Meat is a scarcity, however. Once this summer we had a ham which a kind friend brought in, and even slicing it very small it was hard to make it go round to one hundred and twenty-five people. None of the fellows who were cooking in the kitchen had any. I came up at the tail end of the dinner. Stanley Vishnewski had finished the spiritual reading, "In the Footsteps of Saint Francis," and was sitting down to a meatless plate. The boys had saved a piece for me and there was applesauce and mashed potatoes besides. Oblivious to Stanley's lack I was digging in with great enjoyment.

And then there came a wail from the kitchen. "No meat for me? And I've been working all day! I don't see how everybody else rates meat, and not me. Those that hang around and do nothing get the best food, and me, I went on an errand and so I get left."

The querulous tones went on. The fellow came in, looking sadly at his plate; slammed it on the table and sat down. "I been smelling that all afternoon, too. I just *wanted* a piece of ham."

I offered him half of mine, Ed Kelleher, who used to be a house detective, and a gentle, holy soul he is, too, offered him his.

"I don't eat off nobody's plate," the hungry one said. "But I did want a piece of that ham." A great tear rolled down his nose.

It is incidents like this that break your heart, sometimes. There is never enough food to go around. The pots are always being scraped so clean it is a wonder the enamel doesn't come off. There never is anything in the Electrolux ice box we bought for fifty dollars from the baker around the corner, five dollars down and five dollars once in a while. He gives us a lot of free bread and rolls, too.

Meals are so important. The disciples knew Christ in the breaking of bread. We know Christ in each other in the breaking of bread. It is the closest we can ever come to each other, sitting down and eating together. It is unbelievably, poignantly intimate.

## *A good supper*

Last night we had a very good supper. John Kernan and Duncan Chisholm have charge of the kitchen and Shorty is the *sous-chef*. They also have as assistants John Monaghan and Jim O'Hearn. They take charge of the lunch and dinner every day, and another staff, under Peter Clark, takes charge of the eight hundred on the bread line each morning. These hot days nobody wants anything but bread and coffee, and the bread is pumpernickel or rye, good and substantial.

I read some place, I think it was in one of these ten-cent-store children's books on "Wheat," that the gluten in wheat is the nearest thing to human flesh. And it was wheat that Christ chose when He left us His presence on our altars!

Lunch is always simple, a huge vegetable soup and bread. We make about twenty gallons, and it does a thorough job of heating the kitchen these broiling days.

Supper is more elaborate—sometimes we say "dinner." Last week, thanks to a Long Island farmer and the priest who sent him to us, we had a good vegetable supper—potatoes, beets, carrots, cabbage. We had to buy the potatoes off him at seventy-five cents a bushel, but the rest came free. By Sunday we had run out of cabbage and carrots so we had potatoes and beets. As it was Sunday, we had got fifteen pounds of chopped meat, at fifteen cents a pound, and made a meat loaf. There was a goodly amount of bread mixed with it.

### Gravies

John is a genius at making gravies. I doubt the Waldorf-Astoria has better gravies than we do. It was so good a meal, and everybody was so hungry, not having eaten all day, what with the heat, that I became consumed with anxiety as to whether the food was going to stretch for all. The back court seemed to be full of men and women and there were even some children. One woman had walked all the way down from Fifteenth Street with her two-year-old to have a hot meal. Her gas and electric had been turned off and she could not cook. She is on relief and never seems to catch up, she says.

Little Billy ran around the dining room disrupting things between bites, so we moved mother and child out to the kitchen to finish their meal so the line could go on. We can't seat more than twenty-five and there have to be six sittings. I had finished early and begun hovering over the pots on the stove. John kept counting the men on the line. "Thirty-six more to go," he groaned as he sliced down the last of the meat loaf. Soon he was putting the scraps in the gravy and began contemplating *that*.

"Get me the gravy-stretcher," he called to Shorty; and Shorty, always willing, began to scurry about the kitchen, proffering him one utensil after another. (I one day asked Shorty if he had any relatives, and he said mournfully, "I had a mother once.")

Finally it dawned on him that it was a bit more hot water John wanted to stretch the gravy with, and he brought it. Then a bowlful of boiled potatoes was discovered and they were peeled and dumped into the frying pans. John believes in having things nice.

"Eighteen left to go," Monaghan said as he leaned out the window and looked. And then suddenly five more women, from the Salvation Army hotel on Rivington Street, came in and threw our calculations out again. (Women are always served first and the men step to one side to let them get by.)

"Eight more coming up," and by this time the mashed potatoes were gone and fried potatoes were being dished up.

Thank God there was still plenty of good gravy, and there were some chunks of meat in it too. Not a speck came back on the plates. They were all wiped clean with bits of bread.

And then the last one was served, and there was exactly one helping left! The dishes were being done as we went along, the pots were all cleaned, and there remained only the tables to swab off and the kitchen and dining room to sweep, and we were done.

The one helping was put away in the icebox (and Julia came in around ten and had not eaten since lunch); and then everyone went out of the hot house to the street, where all the neighbors sit in rows along the house-fronts and along the curb and there are card games going on all the long evening.

Down the street the children had turned on a fire hydrant and flung a barrel over it, a headless barrel, and the water cascaded into the air thirty feet like a fountain. The sound was pleasant and so were the cheers of the children as they rushed through the deluge. Little boys paddled "boats" in the rushing curb-streams. Shopkeepers deflected the water onto their sidewalks and began sweeping, and mothers moved their baby carriages out of the flood. All the little boys and some of the little girls got their feet soaked.

Down the street came a singer with his accordion and the happy sound of Italian love songs accompanied the rushing sound of our sudden city streams.

John and Jim of the kitchen sat and rested and there was a look of happy content on their faces. They are both jobless, and are volunteers in the work of our Catholic Worker Community; there is war in the world and they are faced with conscription and little else in the way of security for the future. But it was a fine happy evening and it had been a very good meal.

# About Mary                                          **20**

---

T HIS MORNING after Communion I thought of writing about Mary, and since the thought came to me at *that* time, I took it as an order. I always say to the Blessed Mother after Communion—"Here He is in my heart; I believe, help thou mine unbelief; adore Him, thank Him and love Him for me. He is your Son; His honor is in your hands. Do not let me dishonor Him."

And since too at that moment came this thought, those glimpses of all she has meant to me,—all the little contacts with her that brought me to Him,—I felt I must write.

One of the reasons I do not write more is that there is always house-work, cleaning, scrubbing, sewing, washing (right now it is cleaning fish), etc., to do. Just as she had to do these things, and probably never neglected them. But then too I can see her sitting seemingly idle beside a well on just such a day as this, just thanking Him, with each happy breath.

~

Down in New Orleans twenty years ago I was working for the *Item*, an afternoon paper, and the job was not a very satisfactory one. Women writers, "girl reporters," had to write feature stuff. I started in writing a

Originally published in *Commonweal*, November 5, 1943. Vol. XXXIX, 62–3.

column about homely things—the same kind of a column I write now—
the "Day after Day" column, in *The Catholic Worker*. But they soon gave
me assignments, some good, some bad. I had to interview Jack Dempsey,
and such like, visiting celebrities. Once I had to cover the political situation and write a series of interviews with the retiring governor and the
newly-elected governor of the state. I had to work in a dance hall for a
week as a taxi dancer and write a series of articles, in one of which I
insulted, so they said, the United States Navy. Representatives from the
sailors of a battleship in port at the time came to the newspaper office
to rebuke me. It was a change from the work I had been doing in
Chicago in the radical movement. But I didn't like it much.

Across the street from where I lived, I think it was on St. Peter Street,
there was the side entrance to the cathedral. Every night I used to go in
there for Benediction. Perhaps I was influenced by reading the novels of
Huysmans that I had borrowed from Sam Putnam's library in Chicago.
My roommate was Mary Gordon (when I last heard of her, she was
working for the League for Spanish Democracy in Chicago, a Communist affiliate), and that Christmas she gave me a rosary. So in this case
I was led to the Church through two Communists. I did not know how
to say the rosary, but I got a little prayer book at a Catholic book store
which I often visited, and I learned how. Once in a while I said it. I remember expressing the desire to talk to a priest—to the girl who ran
the book shop—but nothing came of it.

~

My first statue of the Blessed Mother. Peggy was my roommate in
jail in Washington. When we were in the Occoquan workhouse we had
adjoining rooms. In the Washington city jail I had the upper berth on
one of the upper tiers, and Peggy had the lower. I read the Bible and
she wrote a book of poetry—"Poems to My Lovers," she called it. I also
read letters from the boys I was going with at the time, one of them, my
most regular correspondent, a United States sailor. It was during the
last war. Some years afterward Peggy gave me a little statue of the
Blessed Mother which had been brought from Czechoslovakia. It was
made of wax, and very delicate, and there was a golden watchspring-
like halo around its head, and golden curly hair and a bright blue robe.
How I loved that statue! Down in Staten Island in my little shore
cottage I kept it on a shelf by the door with a vigil light burning in front
of it.

Peggy also was a member of the Communist party at different times, but being an undisciplined creature and an artist I don't think she was a paid-up member for long.

~

One summer right after I became a Catholic I was taking care of a number of little boys from a school "for individual development." Together with Freda, my next-door neighbor, whose friend it was who ran the school, we took the responsibility for about a dozen boys between eight and twelve. Quite a few of them were children of Communist parents, and several of them have grown up now to be members of the Young Communist League. I used to read them the "Little Flowers of Saint Francis," which they enjoyed immensely, and they used to command each other "in the name of holy obedience" to perform this or that act of mischief. They also used to ask me to burn candles for them before the little blue statue of the Blessed Mother. Do any of them remember her now?

~

When my daughter was born almost eighteen years ago, I turned her over to the Blessed Mother. "What kind of a mother am I going to be?" I kept thinking to myself. "What kind of a Catholic home is she going to have, with only me?" And with the Catholic Worker movement starting six years later the home problem was even more acute.

There was a solution of course to such a difficulty. "You," I told the Blessed Mother, "will have to be her mother. Under the best of circumstances I'm a failure as a homemaker. I'm untidy, inconsistent, undisciplined, temperamental, and I have to pray hard every day for final perseverance."

It is only these last few years that it has occurred to me why my daughter has never called me "mother." From the time she first spoke, it was "Dorothy." I'd think—"of course with no other children around calling me 'mother' it is natural for her to call me by my first name." I'd correct her but it did no good. Later on I'd ask her, "How will anyone know I'm your mother if you do not call me 'mother'? They'll think I adopted you. They'll think I'm your aunt or something." "I don't care," she would say firmly, "I just can't call you 'mother.'" And for a child really extremely obedient, it was hard to understand such stubbornness.

Once, in the little post office on Staten Island—she was four then—the postmistress said, "I'd like to hear a child of mine call me by my first name! I'd give it to her!"

When she was in convent school her brief letters began *"Dear Mother,"* but it was under compulsion. The Sisters would not let her write unless she so began. But away from school, the letters continue, "Dear Dorothy."

And then a few years ago, it came like a flash of light, "The Blessed Virgin Mary is Mother of my child. No harm can ever come to her with such a Mother."

# Tobacco Road                                    **21**

---

THE STORY BEGINS with my speaking at downtown Fordham to the Sodality of Our Lady, one noon hour some years ago. The meeting had a note in the *Times* perhaps, under "Meetings of the Day," and that's how some outsiders happened to be there.

I talked of the Green Revolution, and how Lenin had said that there could be no revolution without a theory of revolution, and how students had taken a vital part in movements in other countries, and how the Fordham students could not only be studying the theory of the Green Revolution, but also be participants, spreading Catholic periodicals and pamphlets as the Communists did. I pointed out how, in times of change, newspapers were always suppressed; how Trotsky was first sent to Siberia for distributing leaflets outside a factory in Odessa. (I indulged in these radical examples not only because of my former Communist associations, but because if makes the students feel the more keenly their own complacent attitude of taking things for granted).

I finished my talk by asking the students to do as much as they could in spreading Catholic periodicals by leaving them in subways, buses, trains, on their way to and from school, and also to familiarize themselves with what was going on by reading them.

During the question period a young girl in the rear raised her hand. "I'm not a Fordham student, and I'm not a sodality member," she said. "I'm an actress in 'Tobacco Road.'"

Originally published in *Commonweal,* November 26, 1943. Vol. XXXIX, 140–1.

There was the same kind of stunned silence that always ensues when I speak of Lenin or Trotsky as an example to be followed. Peter Maurin believes in the technique of surprise. He thinks people need to be startled, but I wonder sometimes if we don't startle them too much. There was no doubt about it though, the audience certainly had listened to every word.

"I came here because I saw the meeting advertised," she said, "and I wanted to learn more about *The Catholic Worker*. I first got a copy a few months ago on a very cold day, up on Forty-second Street. I'd passed the fellow who sold the paper many times before, and thought how undignified it was for a Catholic paper to be hawked on the street like that—just as though it were a Communist or a Judge Rutherford sheet. But it was so cold that I felt sorry for the fellow who sold it, and bought a copy.

"And when I read it, I enjoyed it so; I could understand every bit of it. I decided I'd spread it around as much as possible. So I made it my job to go to all the houses in my parish, from door to door, and ask them whether they wanted to subscribe to the *Sunday Visitor*, or *The Catholic Worker*. I gave them their choice, but I made them take one paper. I did that every month all winter. And I like *The Catholic Worker* so much myself, because it deals with people who are poor, that I took if for every member of the cast of 'Tobacco Road.'"

She added a little sadly, a little apologetically, "Of course there is an awful lot of profanity in the play, and a lot of wickedness. But I pray for those poor people, and every time I hear them take the Lord's name in vain I say 'Jesus, Mary and Joseph, forgive them.'"

Ruth Byrnes was there for that meeting and we were going to have lunch together afterward, with one of the priests. We were both touched and charmed by Miss Hunter and invited her to go to lunch with us. She was a completely natural person and we enjoyed the luncheon very much. She had not so much sympathy with some aspects of *The Catholic Worker*, the women's house of hospitality for instance.

"I worked like a dog myself," she told us, "so I don't see why any woman cannot get a job doing housework or something like that. If a woman is not lazy she can always find a home. In between stock company jobs, I always took what I could get, housework or anything else." She told us that she was married, had a child and had built a home with her earnings from "Tobacco Road," and that she was going to give up her job soon.

Also she invited Ruth and me to see the show. Neither of us had ever had any intention of seeing it, but we accepted her offer of seats, so one evening that week we found ourselves in about the sixth row, listening to about as sad a play as any one could conceive.

What was most horrible was the audience. They laughed with delight at every obscenity. They howled in shocked amazement at the bawdy missionary woman, at the antics of the harelipped girl (Miss Hunter). When there was nothing to eat but a turnip, they shouted with laughter over the hunger portrayed. When a Negro was killed, and one of the Southerners said, "It's only a nigger," they laughed at that. They laughed at incest and lechery and hunger and death. And the audience was not just Broadway, not just New York, but people from all over the country.

After the performance we went back to Miss Hunter's dressing room. There was a picture of the Sacred Heart on the wall. She had made tea for us, and there was a box of little cookies which she had made herself. "Well, I could see how shocked you were," she said sadly, as she got herself into her clothes. "It *is* awful, isn't it? It started out as a pretty serious show, but every time some line got a laugh, we had to step up the action, play up the aspect that the audience wanted. I've always taken the show seriously. I've prayed for those poor ones. They have one appetite they can satisfy, and only one, and they satisfy it the only way they can. They are hungry and Godforsaken. Even their land is being taken from them, worn out as it is. They have nothing left but sex. They are a degraded lot and there's lots of poor like that too, and who are we to be passing judgment."

"Perhaps it always was bawdy. But also it was a serious play. It was the audience that made it what it is."

# Review:
## *In the Steps of Moses*

**22**

---

In the Steps of Moses *by Louis Golding. Jewish Publication Society of America.* $2.50.

W HEN I READ first the story of Moses in Father Knox's abridged Bible without all the geneologies, the laws, the offerings prescribed for making the tabernacle and its appurtenances and the descriptions of the vestments of the priests which interrupt that epic, I was breathless with the realization that there again was pictured the age-old problem of human freedom and responsibility, of leadership and dictatorship.

I had started study of the laws of the Old Testament some years before because of Peter Maurin's insistence on the teaching of the Fathers of Israel and the Fathers of the Church as being the basis for social reconstruction (the teaching on usury, the moratorium, and the Year of Jubilee, for instance). But one gets the story of Moses best in the Knox edition.

Louis Golding's book is a welcome addition to my knowledge of the Prophet and the places of his wandering. The story of Moses was familiar to Mr. Golding from the kitchen of his Jewish home at Doomington, England, years ago when his father traced the journey on a chart, framed in maple wood on the dark wall. The flavor of that background

Originally published in *Commonweal*, December 17, 1943. Vol. XXXIX, 237–8.

is all through the book, even in the awesome, rigid and foreign atmosphere of the Convent of Mt. Sinai where the travelers stayed during their time on that holy mountain.

The story begins in Egypt and Mr. Golding brings to bear on his account, not only his knowledge of the Bible, but of the Talmud, Jewish folklore and tradition. He searches for the birthplace of Moses near the Nile, he tells of Joseph's account of the early life of Moses. He fought for Pharaoh in a war against Ethiopia, there gaining the experience which helped him in his campaigns against the foe on the way to the promised land. He married a Cushite (Ethiopian woman) "most devoutly believed by the Negroes of America who take great pride in the thought that the Lawgiver took himself a wife out of the black people." (I had never heard this before.) He tells of the crossing of the Red Sea, the journey to Sinai, and the long and weary journeyings in the wilderness.

In keeping up with the archeologists Mr. Golding is often too scholarly for the general reader. Whether Mt. Hor is at Jebel Harum or at Gebel Madra, and whether there is a similarity of names between Madra and Moseroth, or whether it is at Gebel Moweeilleh, some twelve and one-half miles north of Ain Kadeis—and whether Petra and Kadeshbarnea are the same place—these endless discussions become very wearisome and there are pages and pages of them.

But there are exciting accounts, too, of terrifying trips down mountain tracks that were "small waterfalls and shifting slithers of gravel"; there is the night in the two-room house of Sheikh Suleiman in Dana: wife, ten children, goats, chickens and calves in one room and the guests in the other; the banquet on the mountain side on a ledge looking over an abyss, where they all ate with their hands, from a caldron, of boiled mutten, rice and sour milk. These are unforgettable pictures left with you. Both for those who love travel books and for those who love the Bible this book is of deep interest.

# Review:
## *Our Lady of the Birds*

# 23

Our Lady of the Birds *by Louis J. A. Mercier. St. Anthony. $1.25.*

B ROTHER STEPHEN, who had lived in the world a long time and
had thought and studied and worried and read books of philosophy and theology, turned to a Benedictine monastery to find peace and
there goes to work as a lay brother. At first he was happy as he had
never been before; and then in his joy he built a shrine to our Lady, our
Lady of the birds.

Later, when questionings and drynesses and sad distress over that
great question of evil in the world tormented Brother Stephen, our
Lady answers him, through nature itself, through his fellow worker
Brother Joseph, and through the Father Prior.

There are profound matters for meditation in this little 68-page
book, most attractively printed and illustrated by Vincent Summers. It
is filled with the sacramentality of life, this story of doubting man,
coming to the realization that "the universe is alive with natural and
supernatural life in an intertwined symphony."

Its last pages have the refrain, "God is love, and only love can make
us like unto God." "Even now we are in heaven or hell, according to
the measure of our love."

Originally published in *Commonweal*, January 14, 1944. Vol. XXXIX, 332.

# Peter and Women                    24

---

Fragment from an unpublished manuscript.

---

THERE HAS BEEN a faithful friend of Peter whom I would like to write about, Lillian Weiss, who has been a devoted follower of his since our paper first was published back in 1933. She is a convert from Judaism who earns her living by cooking and housework. Out of her wages, she has bought Peter eyeglasses, clothes, shoes, suits—and because she has always been poor too, her gifts have come from rummage sales and secondhand shops.

She is one of those I think of with respect for her poverty, her hardships, and her life of hard work.

Here is part of a letter she wrote once to Peter. It was after she had known him for three years that she ventured to speak of herself:

"May I border on the personal for a few minutes, hoping I will not prove a bore, to state only one incident of God's protection? As a child of not quite fifteen, a speaker at a Protestant mission I went to, advised us all to own a New Testament, which I had the fortune to purchase soon after in pin type and small size for a few cents at a secondhand bookstore. I read the accounts of the sacred passion of Christ in the different gospels, alone, at the top of a hill in Central Park at 106th Street, and felt keenly for the suffering of Christ in my gospel meditations, and concealed the small-size Testament in my stocking when home,

Originally published in *Commonweal*, December 6, 1946. Vol. XLV, 188–91.

and at night under my pillow on the black leather couch in the kitchen where I slept.

"For Labor Day I had an appointment with a girl chum Fanny but at daybreak my father who chanced into the kitchen, found my Testament on the floor beside me, and at once aroused my mother with the find. She awoke me and ordered me out of her house at once, forbidding me to comb or wash, told me not go near my sister, and she sent me forth into the early break of day saying, 'You are easily fooled, you'll land into the gutter anyway some day, you might as well go now.'

"I walked from 110th Street to Bronx Park and had a capital of eight cents. I purchased a morning paper for two, but could not qualify to answer any of the ads, and I had nothing to eat since the day before. It was late in the afternoon when I decided to spend my nickel to get the advice of my girl chum. I got off at 116th Street and paused to try to help a woman seated on the steps of a private house to her feet. She was intoxicated and some men took her away. A middle-aged man engaged me in conversation, 'Your eyes are all red; what were you crying about, you're too nice to bother with drunken people.'

"I told him I had been crying because I had no success all day looking for work. He wrote a name on a slip of paper and the address and told me to go right over as his wife needed a companion, but he could not go with me. The job was so easy, he said, and he made me promise I would stop for nothing but go at once, and he shook my hand and then as I skipped along only God took care of me. A woman ran after me, calling 'little girl' a few times until I turned around. 'What did that man say to you?' 'He is sending me to a position.' 'Well, if you go to that position, you'll never see the light of day again. I was sitting at the parlor window with my mother watching you and I said, the devil is in that man, and I wonder what he is saying to that little girl, and I was glad when he went in the opposite direction. Mother said, don't interfere, but I threw my baby in my mother's lap—see, there she is holding my baby, and I flew out after you.'

"Yes, I have much to thank God for."

$$\sim$$

Peter's idea of a valiant woman, as is that of the Church, is the picture of the holy woman, portrayed in the thirty-first Book of Proverbs:

> *Who shall find a valiant woman?*
> *Far and from the uttermost coasts is the price of her.*

*The heart of her husband trusteth in her;*
*And he shall have no need of spoils.*
*She will render him good and not evil*
*All the days of her life.*
*She hath sought wool and flax,*
*And hath wrought by the counsel of her hands.*
*She is like the merchant's ship;*
*She bringeth her bread from afar,*
*And she has risen in the night, and given a prey to her household,*
*And victuals to her maidens.*
*She hath considered a field and bought it*
*With the fruit of her hand she hath planted a vineyard.*

*She hath girded her loins with strength*
*And hath strengthened her arm*
*She hath tasted and seen that her traffic is good.*
*Her lamp shall not be put out by night.*
*She hath put out her hand to strong things;*
*And her fingers hath taken hold of its spindle.*

*She hath opened her hands to the needy*
*And stretched out her hands to the poor.*
*She shall not fear for her house in the cold of snow;*
*For her domestics are clothed with double garments.*
*She hath made for herself clothing of tapestry;*
*Fine linen and purple is her covering.*
*Her husband is honorable in the gates,*
*When he sitteth among the senators of the land.*
*She made fine linen and sold it, and delivered a girdle to the Canaanite.*
*Strength and beauty are her clothing*
*And she shall laugh in the latter day.*

*She hath opened her mouth to wisdom;*
*And the law of clemency is on her tongue.*
*She hath looked well to the paths of her house,*
*And hath not eaten her bread idle.*
*Her children rose up and called her blessed.*
*Her husband, and he praiseth her.*

*Many daughters have gathered together riches;*
*But thou has surpassed them all.*
*Favor is deceitful and beauty is vain;*
*The woman that feareth the Lord, she shall be praised.*
*Give her of the fruit of her hands;*
*And let her works praise her in the gates.*

This of course is the picture of a queen, sung by her son Lemuel, but Peter would apply it to a woman in the slums, to a peasant woman on the land.

The poem depicts Peter's vision of a philosophy of labor, of love and joy in work, a sense of the beauty of work. It clearly emphasizes the sense of personal responsibility, the practice of the Works of Mercy, the care for others around her, the selflessness of the mother of a household.

In discussing women Peter always gets back to his thesis that people in the cities are cut off from the sources of life by the urban cultural pattern.

All great civilizations, he points out, have been based on a sound agriculture. The cities of the past have been comparatively small, and represent the flowering of the culture of the countryside.

"Woman is matter, man is spirit," Peter said one time, and none of us understood him.

But he was thinking of woman and her nature which is so close to the sources of life, most completely herself when she is caring for growing things, providing for them, feeding them, clothing them. It is not an empty phrase—"Mother Earth," fecund, warm, rich, constant and silent.

Meditating on these things, one begins to understand what Peter means when he says "woman is matter." Unless she uses her body to produce and her hands to serve her young, she is unfulfilled, undeveloped, stunted and thwarted.

The valiant woman was strong—she put her hand to strong things. She bore burdens, she worked late, "she hath risen in the night," "her lamp shall not be put out." Yet always strong, healthy—"she hath strengthened her arm, she hath tasted and seen that her traffic is good."

The peculiar lack of balance in our present-day living is epitomized for Peter by the fact that the rich, who have earned their money by factories, value only the "handmade."

"You too can be rich," cries Peter, "you too can put your hands to the crafts, furnish homes, weave and spin, bake bread. Then you will value what you have produced. Then you will put *yourself* into it. Then you will have given yourself. Then you will begin to understand the sacramentality of life. You will understand the sacramental principle, you will begin to see God in all things. You will look upon what God has made, and find it good. You will look at things as God looks at them. You will begin to have the mentality of sons of God, daughters of God."

~

In the ten years we have been exercising personal responsibility and taking in the homeless in New York, there have been many women coming to us, and one of the things that always astounded me about them was that they represented to a fearful degree, the ravages of our industrial life. Of course we got the worst of cases, to use a horrid word. We got girls who had been factory workers, chambermaids, restaurant and office workers, girls who had been working in industry from their earliest childhood, who had come from bad homes of the grossest materialism, the kind of materialism which had no respect for the material of life. They did not know how to cook, nor sew, and at the best they were able, painfully, to do a little cleaning. They certainly had little joy in their work. It was all drudgery to them. They suffered from many ailments, from bad food, from worry, from insufficient sleep. They suffered from fear.

Beatrice provided for us, I always thought, an extreme example of the rootless woman. She and her sister had come from Ireland just before the depression; when her sister got work as a traveling saleswoman, Beatrice found work as a chambermaid. Then during the depression she found nothing, or at least nothing she wanted to do, or could do. I do not see how she could have done housework myself, because once when she was doing some cleaning she put water on the stove to heat in a wooden bucket. Another time she was given a very good dress, a woolen suit from Peck and Peck, which one of our friends had sent in, and the next week I found Beatrice using the skirt of it for a mop cloth. Whether she did this deliberately to show her contempt for the charity of the rich, I do not know. She was a beautiful young thing with a queenly and scornful air.

I used to worry about her a good deal because she was so beautiful and so reckless. When she could not sleep at night she used to get up at two o'clock in the morning and walk across Manhattan bridge. She was a creature of impulse and energy and became very impatient with those on the farm who sat and talked of building houses and never got anywhere with it.

"If you want to build, why don't you start? Why don't you dig? I could start to build a house this morning."

Everyone laughed at her, but after breakfast she went out, found tools for herself, and started digging. She picked a spot at random, between the main house and the chicken coop, well within the sight of all, and spent the entire morning digging with pickax and spade and by noon a sizable hole was done.

She left off at noon, and aside from the comments, "Did you see what that crazy Beatrice was doing all morning?" there was no other comment on her labor. Except perhaps to criticize the spot chosen for a house. Did she have a point in this strange display of energy? If so it was quite lost on the young men who sat around talking about building.

She was a literal creature, and once one of the men who had come to New York from the Boston house of hospitality, mentioned that there was a violin in the Boston house, which she could have if she wished. She left the lunch table in New York and was not seen for a few days. When she walked in not many nights after, she reported, "there is no violin up there," and sat down to eat. She had hitchhiked to Boston, with not a cent of money in her pocket, made her inquiry and hitchhiked back again.

She had spent several years with us, trying to be useful by mopping floors and painting when she could lay her hands on the paint. Whenever anyone was in the way of her painting and would not move, she went right on painting right over their shoes.

Then suddenly her sister showed up at the house and insisted on sending Beatrice back to Ireland. Every now and then we heard from her. She missed the excitement, she wrote, of Mott Street. (A good deal of that excitement she made.) Since the war there has been silence.

Beatrice is just one of many women we have had to deal with. There have been feeble-minded women—a woman who sat in her room with a towel tied about her nose with the plaint that there was poison gas in the room. There have been women addicted to drink. There have been women of all nations, Japanese, Chinese, Lithuanian, Russian, Polish, German, Italian, Jews, English, Irish, colored women. There have been working women and intellectual women, but when I try to find a valiant woman amongst them, I search in vain.

~

As I write, thinking back into the past, I do remember such a woman— I met her years ago on the island of Capri, just outside the village of Anacapri. She was the wife of the mayor of the little town, a Norwegian, I believe, and she was a woman of culture and gentleness and beauty. She could play the piano and the harp. The shelves of her library were covered with the books she had read. Her walls were hung with tapestries, her furniture upholstered with what she had made. She was a wood carver, she could spin and weave. She made her wine, she dried her fruits, she salted down the anchovies her husband's fishermen brought in. She managed her large household and ministered to the poor.

And there are valiant women, and the makings of valiant women with us here in the United States. These are women with an integrated outlook on life, who correlate the material and the spiritual, who understand what Peter is talking about when he discourses on "the soul of woman."

# Letter: Things Worth Fighting For?                   25

TO THE EDITORS: This is one of those questions which good people put to you. And they mean, "worth fighting and dying for." Not just worth dying for. But what are those things?

Our Faith? That is what they mean. But are they thinking of that? In Arabia, the American oil companies now have concessions up to the year 2000. They are getting so much oil that they say they can supply all their foreign markets and have enough left for home. In order to get this oil, they have given up their religion. The colony of American workers, their wives, children, of the American oil companies, together with the United States Air Force and its families have all given up Sunday in order to keep the good will of the Arabs. They work Saturdays and Sundays and take Thursday afternoon and Friday off. They have neither chapel nor chaplain.

These representatives of America, both army and commercial, have already given up their God, have sold their Christ, in order to have "the good will of the Arabs." So don't let us talk anymore of saving our faith when we beat the drums for a war with Russia. It is a war between empires, and neither of them is Christian.

War is deviltry. It calls for sacrifices indeed, but not at the altar of love. "Greater love hath no man than this." A great blasphemy this, to use Christ's words in connection with men going to war. They go because they are drafted, because they are afraid of what their neighbors will say, because the pay is good, because the benefits accruing afterward (the G.I. Bill of Rights) are great. And they are told by press and

Originally published in *Commonweal*, May 21, 1948. Vol. XLVIII, 136–7.

pulpit that they are going because they love their fellows, and they are filled with a warm glow of self-love. And then they are given their intensive training in how to escape death, how to kill.

Greater love hath no man than this, that he lay down his life for his brothers, and the Russians are our brothers, the Negro is our brother, the Japanese are our brothers, the Germans, the Mexicans, the Filipinos, the Jews, the Arabs.

The Italian Victory is not a victory. It is a postponement. The Church, the faithful, have not yet met the challenge. Christian democrats achieved their ends by the threat of force, by the threat of civil war, by a tremendous show of force at the polls, armed force, not just the force of the cloister and the hearth. We have not yet paid the price of peace, given up the friendship, love, esteem of the world. The folly of the cross. We do not yet know what it means. Loving our enemy. We only fear him. We have great possessions, like the young man in the gospel and we turn from Christ to the use of force to protect them. Not our Church, our school, our home. We have given up our Church in Arabia (it is an example). We have secularized our schools "they are just as good as the public schools" (just as bad) and we have no homes (see figures on divorce and juvenile delinquency). We are losing the battle at home, without the Russians lifting a finger.

So let's not have any more talk about God and country. The battle is for this world, for the possessions of this world.

*This letter puts everything in question once more, and naturally so because Dorothy Day wrote it, and her contemporaries have learned to expect from her no compromise, no acceptance of hate, no deviation from what she considers the demands of absolute justice and charity. That is why we cannot conceal our surprise at the passage in which she lists the reasons—all blindly selfish—for which men go to war. That passage reflects an automatism, a determinism unworthy of her thinking and style; it could have been written by one who knew nothing of the human heart and who denied the soul. It could not have been written by Charles Péguy; perhaps it should not have been written by Dorothy Day.*

C.G.P.

[C. G. Paulding was *Commonweal*'s Managing Editor at the time.]

# The Scandal of the Works of Mercy  26

---

To reach the man in the street you must go to the street, where
Christianity itself may be a sign of contradiction.

---

THE SPIRITUAL works of mercy are: to admonish the sinner, to in-
struct the ignorant, to counsel the doubtful, to comfort the sorrowful, to bear wrongs patiently, to forgive all injuries, and to pray for the
living and the dead.

The corporal works are to feed the hungry, to give drink to the thirsty,
to clothe the naked, to ransom the captive, to harbor the harborless, to
visit the sick, and to bury the dead.

When Peter Maurin talked about the necessity of practicing the
works of mercy, he meant all of them, and he envisioned houses of hospitality in poor parishes in every city of the country, where these precepts of Our Lord could be put into effect. He pointed out that we have
turned to State responsibility through home relief, social legislation
and social security, and we no longer practice personal responsibility
for our brother, but are repeating the words of the first murderer, "Am
I my brother's keeper?" Not that our passing the buck is as crude as all
that. It was a matter of social enlightenment, Holy Mother the City
taking over, Holy Mother the State taking the poor to herself, gathering
them to her capacious bosom studded with the jewels of the taxation of

Originally published in *Commonweal*, November 4, 1949. Vol. LI, 99–102.

the rich and the poor alike, the subtle war between Church and State meanwhile going on at all times, in the field of education, charity, the family. In the last fifteen years the all-encroaching State, as the Bishops of the United States have called it, has gained the upper hand.

In our fight against such a concept of Christian charity, we have been accused of lining up with Wall Street and private enterprise, and the rich opponents of state control and taxation. But, anarchists that we are, we want to decentralize everything and delegate to smaller bodies and groups what can be done far more humanly and responsibly through mutual aid, as well as charity, through Blue Cross, Red Cross, union cooperation, parish cooperation.

Peter Maurin, the founder of *The Catholic Worker,* was very much an apostle to the world today, not only to the poor. He was a prophet with a social message and he wanted to reach the people with it. To get to the people, he pointed out it was necessary to embrace voluntary poverty, to strip yourself, which would give you the *means* to practice the works of mercy. To reach the man in the street you must go to the street. To reach the workers, you begin to study a philosophy of labor, and take up manual labor, useful labor, instead of white collar work. To be the least, to be the worker, to be poor, to take the lowest place and thus be the spark which would set afire the love of men towards each other and to God (and we can only show our love for God by our love for our fellows). These were Peter's ideas, and they are indispensable for the performing of the works of mercy.

When Father Lombardi spoke a few weeks ago in St. Patrick's Cathedral and on the Fordham campus, he spoke of the need to make a new social order. He was making no anti-Communist speech, he said. He was making no nationalist speech. He was speaking a gospel of love, and that meant here and now a redistribution of this world's goods, so that a man could have as many children as God sent him, and support them, have a home for them and work for them to do. This world's goods do not belong to any one nation, any few men, he pointed out.

~

We are all devoured by a passion for social justice today, and seeking an alternative to communism and capitalism. We like to discuss capitalism, industrialism, distributism, decentralization—all the work that is being done by the National Catholic Welfare Conference in Washington and by the National Catholic Rural Life Conference, but with this tremendous work of indoctrination, with all this work which goes on in conference, convention, classroom, and through periodicals, much of it comes to words and not very vital words at that.

Peter liked to talk of making a message dynamic, and that meant with him putting it into practice. There was simple common sense in his argument that if you wanted to reach the man in the street, you go out on a park bench with him, you go out to sell your paper on the street just as the Jehovah's Witnesses do, just as the Communists do.

Publishing a paper and reaching the man in the street, was to Peter, performing the first four of the spiritual works of mercy. To go on picket lines, was to perform spiritual works of mercy. It was to dramatize by a supplicatory procession the needs of the worker, the injustice perpetrated against him. To bear wrongs patiently, yes, but not to let the bosses continue in the sin of exploiting you. To forgive the injury, yes, but to try to do away with the injury.

I remember one time when we were all picketing in the National Biscuit Company strike on West Fourteenth Street. There was a mass picket line which extended around the block, and the police began to break it up, and then the scabs arrived in taxi cabs and the mob started to boo, and the whole affair began to look ugly. As we gave out our literature, Frank O'Donnell, who is now one of the members of the farming community at St. Benedict's Farm at Upton, Mass., turned to us all and said mildly, winking at Peter, "Don't forget we are all gentle personalities!"

It reminded me of the Communist who shouted at me as we were dispersed by the police at another demonstration, and there was a brutal show of force by the police: "What about a little brotherly love, sister?"

Yes, such works of mercy, such spiritual works of mercy, can be dangerous, and can smack of class war attitudes. And of that we are often accused, because the performance of the works of mercy finds us on the side of the poor, the exploited, whether with literature, picketing, soup kitchen, etc. As Evelyn Waugh said to us plaintively last spring, "Don't you think the rich suffer too?" And there is indeed plenty of room for the works of mercy there. Perhaps we are also carrying out that apostolate too. Perhaps some of the rich are reading *The Catholic Worker*. After all, *Commonweal* must have readers who are able to afford the things advertised in its columns, such as jewels, laces and fur coats, which puts them definitely out of the class of the Fourteenth Street reader and shopper whom we cater to.

~

We are always accused of going to extremes and perhaps it does seem like an extreme to be talking of the street apostolate and the retreat apostolate in the same breath. Yet they go together. In the attempt to perform these works of mercy, which are far more difficult than the immediate physical ones of feeding and clothing and sheltering, we came to the decision after ten years of work in city and country throughout the land that we needed a retreat house for the work. We had had colloquiums for the clarification of thought, and tired of wrangling, we had tried an annual retreat for all the leaders of the Catholic Worker Houses in the United States; so many came, and the response was so great, that we decided to have a year-round retreat house where we could raise what we needed as much as possible, where we could build up our very good library, where we could have a house of studies for those who wanted to stay longer than the week's retreat on the farm.

The first project was at Easton, and never was there such a retreat house. Generous priests gave us their time, and came and slept in unheated rooms and dormitories. At first there was no running water, but one valiant priest, Father Pacifique Roy, s.s.j., who had been a missionary both in Quebec and Louisiana and accustomed to working with his hands, directed the work by example as well as by precept, and we dug ditches and laid pipe and soon had running water on every floor of the barn and the house. We had electricity in every room, and the electrical work was done by Father Roy and our men. During the war, when it was all but impossible to get men or materials, we had the genius of this priest who knew how to use all odds and ends of pipe and wire and make up gadgets to take the place of those we could not get. If Father Roy could have been spared to us (he is invalided in Canada right now) we would have had a lumber mill, a cement block plant and a grist mill and electricity from our own windmill, and all such contrivances of human ingenuity for our farm retreat house.

As it is, we have become more bourgeois and comfortable, but not more self-sufficient. We have a long way to go to exemplify the poverty of a St. Francis or a Peter Maurin.

People out of jails and out of hospitals, men from the breadline and from the road, readers of the paper from all walks of life, students, priests too, come to make retreats with us. We have a chapel in which the stations of the cross, the statues of the Blessed Mother and St. Joseph are made by our own artists. Adé de Bethune carved the crucifix over the altar, and the altar and the benches were made by one of the men who came in from the Bowery, an old carpenter with a bitter tongue, who so despised the unskilled poor that whenever anyone gave any evidence of any skill, he would say sourly, "And what jail did you learn that in?"

This old man nearing eighty had his little shop and house right at the entrance to our farm at Easton, where we first had retreats, and unlike the porter at the gate described by St. Benedict, old Maurice had quite a different tongue. I used to feel sad that instead of seeing Christ in each guest who came, he saw the bum, and so treated us, one and all. He was a good example of "The Friend of the Family," "The Man Who Came to Dinner." And also a fitting member of our community, which is country-wide by now, and which Stanley Vishnewski has come to call *"the contemptibles."* "It is a new order I started," he is going around saying. But it is really Peter Maurin who started it. Stanley just named it.

∼

Our retreat house now is at Newburgh, New York, sixty-five miles up the Hudson River and although we are not permanent there, I wish to write about it in some detail, because I have written two other articles for *Commonweal* on the houses of hospitality where works of mercy are performed.

We are intending to sell the place at Newburgh and buy one on some bay near New York where we can fish and so cut down our expenses. Fishing and clamming and beachcombing are occupations more agreeable to man than farming. We want a twenty acre place so that we can have a large garden and orchard. We do not need the ninety-six acres we have now at Newburgh. We had offered the opportunity to three couples to build there on our acreage, but the offer was not taken up because of the cost of building materials and the lack of skills among the men. Also, because most of those who are contemplating the land movement are still thinking in terms of farms that "pay," whereas we are thinking of a village and town economy and a combination of land and crafts, and the use of the machine only insofar as it is the extension of the hand of man and so under his control, making things of use to others; in other words, a political economy based on the consumers' needs rather than the producers' profits.

It will be seen that our concept of the works of mercy, including as it does making the kind of society where the "rich man becomes poor, and the poor holy," a society where there is no unemployment, and where each can "work according to his ability and receive according to his need," is a foretaste of heaven indeed.

We have had retreats every other week these past two years at Maryfarm, Newburgh, and in the winter when we are limited to the house alone and have to give up the barns and the carriage house and the tents, then the house becomes a rest house as well as a house of studies, and there are always those out of hospitals who need rest and care, sicknesses of mind and body that need to be nursed.

We have daily Mass at the Farm, and we are permitted by the Chancery Office to have the Blessed Sacrament at all times while a priest is with us and we are blessed in having an invalided priest visiting us these past fifteen months or so. We have Prime and Compline, we have sung Masses for all the big feast days, we have readings at the table during retreats, and sometimes when there is no retreat but a feast day to be celebrated. There are many visitors, and it is very much a crowded inn and hospice during all the months of the year. Jane O'Donnell is in charge of the House, and John Filliger of the Farm, and Hans Tunnesen takes care of cooking and carpentry alternately. Both the latter are seamen and have been with us for years. I remember the gibe (a friendly one) of one of our friends once who was combatting our idea of farming communes where the family could enjoy a combination of private and communal property. "Instead of a family commune," he said, "they are running a home for celibate seamen." This was at the time of the first seamen's strike and many were staying with us.

There are families among us who do not have much time for many of the works of mercy any longer outside their own families, though they are always contributors of food and clothing to our community of contemptibles. And it is indeed true that there are many celibates, willing and unwilling ones, among us. Converts come to work with us who might have preferred family life but are barred from it by a previous bad marriage. There will always be, in a way, the willing and the reluctant celibates, and for these, the community life of *The Catholic Worker*, with its men and women working together, dedicated to the common effort, affords the comfort of a home, of contacts with friends, the normal, happy relationships of men and women working together. (The men become more gentle and the women try harder to please, and in spite of the war of sexes which goes on and always will, there is a growth of the good love of friendship so sadly needed in the world today.)

The works of mercy are a wonderful stimulus to our growth in faith as well as in love. Our faith is taxed to the utmost and so grows through this strain put upon it. It is pruned again and again, and springs up bearing much fruit. For anyone starting to live literally the words of the Fathers of the Church, "the bread you retain belongs to the hungry, the dress you lock up is the property of the naked," "what is superfluous for one's need is to be regarded as plunder if one retains it for one's self," there is always a trial ahead. "Our faith, more precious than gold, must be tried as though by fire." Here is a letter we received today. "I took a gentleman seemingly in need of spiritual and temporal guidance into my home on a Sunday afternoon. Let him have a nap on my bed, went through the want ads with him, made coffee and sandwiches for him, and when he left, I found my wallet had gone also."

I can only say that the Saints would only bow their heads and not try to understand or judge. They received no thanks—well then, God had to repay them. They forebore to judge, and it was as though they took off their cloak besides their coat to give away. This is expecting heroic charity of course. But these things happen for our discouragement, for our testing. We are sowing the seed of love, and we are not living in the harvest time so that we can expect a crop. We must love to the point of folly, and we are indeed fools, as our Lord Himself was who died for such a one as this. We lay down our lives too when we have performed so painfully thankless an act, because this correspondent of ours is poor in this world's goods. It is agony to go through such bitter experiences, because we all want to love, we desire with a great longing to love our fellows, and our hearts are often crushed at such rejections. But a Carmelite nun said to me last week, "It is the crushed heart which is the soft heart, the tender heart," and maybe it is one way to become meek and humble of heart like Jesus.

Such an experience is crueller than that of our young men in Baltimore who were arrested for running a disorderly house, i.e., our St. Anthony's house of hospitality, and who spent a few nights in jail. Such an experience is dramatic to say the least. Such an experience is crueller than that which happened to one of our men here in New York who was attacked (for his pacifism) by a maniac with a knife in our kitchen. Actually to shed one's blood is a less bitter experience.

Well, our friend has suffered from his experience and it is part of the bitterness of the poor, who cheat each other, who exploit each other, even as they are exploited. Who despise each other even as they are the despised.

And is it to be expected that virtue and destitution should go together? No, as John Cogley has written, they are the destitute in every way, destitute of this world's goods, destitute of honor, of gratitude, of love, and they need so much, that we cannot take the works of mercy apart, and say I will do this one, or that one work of mercy. We find they all go together.

Some years ago there was an article in *Commonweal* by Georges Bernanos. He ended his article as I shall end mine, paraphrasing his words, and it is a warning note for these apocalyptic times: "Every particle of Christ's divine charity is today more precious for your security—for your security, I say—than all the atom bombs in all the stock piles." It is by the works of mercy that we shall be judged.

# Traveling by Bus

27

You can see the country, meet the people . . . and get where you're going at half the price.

W HERE DO YOU GET all the money to travel around with?" is one of the embarrassing questions asked us when we appear on lecture platforms, and it is asked also in letters from some of the readers of *The Catholic Worker* who disagree with the positions we take. They want to let us know they are judging us severely for spending money which should go to the poor, on jaunting over the highways.

If we write on poverty, and we shall continue to do so, and have others write such articles for *The Catholic Worker* from month to month, it is necessary to meet such questions.

It shows how seriously our readers and listeners take this call to poverty, holy poverty, voluntary poverty, which is the foundation, the starting point of all our work for man's freedom, his dignity and for his love.

Let us say that travel by bus is traveling in poverty but not in destitution. It costs about half as much as by railroad. And as people say who are doing it for the first time, and think they have lowered their standards a little, "you see so much of the country."

I have just returned from a trip to the West Coast, half of which was made by bus. Now that the war is over, you do not have to make

Originally published in *Commonweal*, March 10, 1950. Vol. LI, 577–9.

reservations ahead but can go to the stations half an hour early and get your tickets. The Greyhound of course is the best. The Trailways bus is so built that there is no room for the knees. I have spent a night of misery between New York and Washington, wedged in at the side of a stout woman and with the seat ahead pressing close against me.

Between our farm at Newburgh and New York there are two bus lines operating, the Short Line and the Mohawk. The latter has the more comfortable buses, with reclining seats. But it follows the thrilling, somewhat terrifying road which winds around Bear Mountain and Storm King Mountain. The road is clearly labeled "Dangerous but Passable" and is posted with signs, "Falling Rocks," which cause you to peer up at the jagged cliffs hanging overhead, while you shudder away from the abyss on the other side. The Short Line follows the less picturesque truck route.

There are no dangers between here and the Rockies on the cross-country trip, if you leave out of account fog, sleet and the snow storms at this time of the year. In winter the buses are more crowded because no one can use cars. Between all the little villages along the route people crowd into the buses, smelling of fresh air and snow and talking of conditions back off the highway, of the trucks that are stalled ahead and behind. Just when the radio is warning drivers to keep off the roads I feel safest, because then the cars crawl along and there are fewer of them. I really feel secure in the heavy vehicle that I could never conceivably drive myself, so I don't even have the back-seat driver tendencies that I have in other cars.

We had a good driver leaving New York, cheerful and informative. As we went through the Holland Tunnel he told his passengers all about the explosion which took place in the tunnel some months before. We held our breath, praying, until we got through. Going over the Pulaski Skyway, he said, "This is seven miles long, it took seven years to build, and it cost seven men their lives."

I had heard the same comment about the Golden Gate Bridge. How many lives were lost on these roads, these bridges and tunnels which common men built and dug! You cannot travel by bus without having these ideas impressed upon you, up through the all but impenetrable canyons where power lines have been carried, pipe has been laid, roads have been built, if not stone by stone as in Roman times then actually foot by foot of slow and daily progress from one end of this vast country to the other. It makes you more patient with the slow work you are doing, the small job, the making of meals, the giving out of clothes, the building of that bridge of love from man to man, the creation of a sense of community, fellowship.

This first bus driver stayed with us to Binghamton, I believe, and he was kindly all the way. He allowed plenty of time for rest stops, and counted his passengers whenever he started out again. People have sometimes been left behind by surly bus drivers. One such driver can set the tone of the whole trip, making people grumble and snap at each other. There may be a chain reaction in the mood of the busload, going from the driver to the passengers.

We had one such driver from Chicago to St. Louis, but we found toward the close of the trip that he was suffering from an abscess on the base of his spine and that he could not lay off work to get it attended to, especially around holiday time. Indeed, at the stop where someone was supposed to relieve him, the other driver did not show up, and he was forced to take the bus on into St. Louis. The bus was an old rattle-trap affair that was only put on the route over the holidays. The heater did not work, and one could comfort oneself only by thinking of the stage-coach of Dickens's day. The poor driver was so ill he got out at every stop to be sick, and, though he stopped five or ten minutes, he always snarled at us all that it was not a rest stop, we were not to leave the bus. Towards the close of the evening he broke down and confessed to us all how sick he felt; then he went on with the account of his woe to two men sitting in back of him. He told them of all his troubles with his wife and his mother-in-law. They returned his confidences.

~

Sometimes bus passengers are not the pleasantest of companions. Once in a great while you are afflicted with someone who is a bore and, very rarely, with a real nuisance. I had one such experience in Texas riding from Amarillo to Phoenix. My sufferings became so acute that I had to get off in Albuquerque and wait for the next bus. The problem was an elderly minister (he showed me his card) who confessed that he was running away from his responsibilities. To bolster his courage, he got off at every stop and had a few drinks. I had been visiting a Negro woman in Amarillo who packed me a most elaborate lunch with some delicious roast beef sandwiches. It would have been rude, of course, to eat alone, so I had offered one of the sandwiches to my seat companion. This immediately put us on a footing of intimacy. From then on he became more and more confiding, buying me sandwiches in turn, which

I could not possibly eat, what with the box of lunch I already had. Then when he told me to save them for next day, I foolishly mentioned it was Friday, whereupon I had long sermons and quotations from the Scriptures on man not being saved by meat or drink. At the next stop he bought me a fish sandwich.

As the night wore on my companion was begging me to share a drink with him, always in the most respectful, polite manner, of course. Finally my nerves became so on edge with his persistence that I had to leave the bus and wait over for another. Every seat was taken in the bus we were on, so it was impossible to change seats.

~

Incidents like this, however, are rare. Usually you are in the company of workers, men and women, and they tell you of their jobs, or lack of jobs, their travels, their strivings, and sometimes of their religion.

There was another companion in Texas, a young Bohemian girl, a stenographer in Houston, who had been brought up on the land and was heartbroken to be away from it. Among the travelers there are often truck drivers whose cars have broken down, and they like to stand by the driver and talk of the hazards of the road. Just yesterday, when I was coming down from the farm at Newburgh in a blizzard, the driver of a milk truck came back into the city with me. He had taken his truck as far as Highland Mills and then had to abandon it to be picked up later. All the way down he saw other drivers wrestling with their huge vans and trailers and kept commenting on the struggle. "Mine was an empty, I couldn't do a thing. Now when I get to the city they won't believe me, how bad it is up here. The city's warm and melts the snow." You could feel that it was on his mind that he had not finished his job. He was bothered and resentful at the same time. He was old for a driver and looked worn and battered. His hands were red and chapped and dirty, and he clasped a red Manila folder—his papers, his reports, his job. You felt how much more important than he the job was, the way men have made things today.

Another driver who sat beside me on one of my cross-country trips was a driver of cars from Detroit. He had taken the bus back to get another pair of cars. He described to me how the efficiency "engineers" worked, estimating to the drop the amount of gasoline needed. One time he got behind a parade and the starting and stopping used more gasoline than the experts had estimated so he had a hard time making it to the next stop. Not much chance to pad expense accounts on such jobs. The assumption is that all men are dishonest, and estimates are made accordingly. He explained how the company connived with the driver to get out of paying the special tax in some states, and how they shared the gain.

~

As I traveled across the country this time, I found the buses more crowded than they were a year ago and more people talking about lack of work. "They keep telling us there is no depression," one man grumbled, "but it looks like it's coming on again." The last depression is still in their bones.

Food differs as you go across the United States, though not much in price. In Arkansas and Oklahoma you can get karopecan pie, which is as sweet as Syrian pastry and just as regional. All through the West you should eat chile. It is the cheapest and best dish for a main meal. It isn't the pure Mexican chile, but it's hot enough, and it is the same everywhere, made with red beans and meat and lots of gravy and crackers. A few years ago it was fifteen cents; now it is a quarter. But it is still a full meal and better than anyone can get on a railroad diner.

Yes, we have eaten on diners, and we have traveled in other ways than in buses. When I was coming back from Seattle by the Northern Pacific, by railroad coach, the seating was most comfortable, with wonderful leg rests that made it possible really to sleep soundly all night. But the radio blared all day. No amount of pleading with the porter or conductor would make them turn it off. The Western Pacific with its double-decker sky-view effect was most interesting, but the seating was not so comfortable, and up in the "dome" the fumes of the diesel engine seeped in and the rounded glass was hard on the eyes.

Peter Maurin almost always traveled by buses, but on one occasion someone sent him a railroad ticket to Windsor, Ontario. When we escorted him to the Pullman up at Grand Central, he was not at all at home. The berths were made up, and he was confused by the curtains. He was undoubtedly afraid of getting lost and walking into the wrong bunk.

Peter was much more at home in buses. He was never so happy as when he was setting forth on a trip to speak, to visit our houses of hospitality and farms. Once when we were both speaking at Notre Dame and were leaving the next morning to go in different directions,

Professors Emmanuel Chapman and Robert Pollock accompanied us to the station. They had been enthusiastically arguing with Peter all night and were still going strong that morning. In his absorption in the talk Peter started to get on the wrong bus.

"Look out, Peter, that bus is going to Cincinnati," Pollack cried. Peter answered debonairly, "Oh, that's all right, I know someone there." He was what I would call a real traveler.

# Letter:
# Blood, Sweat and Tears

# 28

TO THE EDITORS: Your editorial (Dec. 15) "Blood, Sweat and Tears" is for me a perfect example of that secularism which the Bishops of the United States in a recent statement deplore as a greater danger than communism. It is an attempt to outline a national defense from the viewpoint of the natural man, untouched by grace, unredeemed. It is also the attempt to speak with the voice of authority, in exalted accents, and except for a beautiful paragraph you quote from Christopher Dawson which seems to belie the rest, it fails to lift up the faltering arms and strengthen the weak knees. It is a cry of distress, of despair almost. It is certainly a cry of fear.

Ignazio Silone said at a Congress in Zurich in 1947: "To be perfectly frank, I do not know if, in recent years, there has been a single country or a single party in which the intellect has not been degraded to the humiliating function of an instrument of war. I assure you, I do not intend to hurt anyone's feelings or to cast the least doubt on the good faith of these writers who at their own risk and peril took part in the ideological war. What I mean to say is, that now the war is over, nobody can deny that the use made by the military leaders of the work of these writers and of the eloquent slogans invented by them was identical with the use made of this or that war weapon. In fact, as soon as there was no more use for them, the principles of liberty, human dignity

Originally published in *Commonweal*, December 29, 1950. Vol. LIII, 300–1.

and universal security were put back into storage just as if they were tanks. That is why we have this peace, which is no peace but at best an uncertain armistice. . . . Never identify the cause of moral value with that of a state. . . . Only by the sacrifice of intellectual honesty is it possible to identify the cause of truth with that of an army."

In time of trouble men turn everywhere but to God, the author of *The Imitation of Christ* writes. It is as though we are saying these days, as it was said at the beginning of the last world war, "This is no time for the beatitudes. This is the time for the militant virtues." All the forces we used then, including the atom bomb, did not bring us peace but built up an ever vaster war.

In the Old Law war was looked upon as a retribution for sin. God always asked for prayer and penance first of all, and He asked too that armies be whittled down to a handful so that His would be the glory. In Deuteronomy rules were laid down for warfare. If men were newly married or had just bought farms or had no desire for war, no talent for it, they were to be sent home. In Maccabees they were even required to be in a state of grace, as it were, free of sin.

Now we have the New Law and we are still disregarding the Old. "Blessed is he who will not be scandalized in Me," Our Lord said in His message to John the Baptist. But we are all scandalized. We see only the failure of the Cross. We have not accepted the folly of the Cross, the humiliated Christ. Now we have begun to be humiliated in Korea. If only we could accept our humiliation in a spirit of penance; if only there is no use of atomic weapons, if only we refrain from a great moral revulsion, not from fear alone, God may save us yet.

～

In the same issue an editorial states that there was no widespread feeling of moral guilt after the bomb was used on Hiroshima. Have the editors so lost faith in the people as to believe that? The legend is that Moses was not permitted to reach the promised land because he wavered in his faith in his people. To lose this faith is not to see Christ in others.

It is time to protest against this horror of war, each one to say no against the acceptance expected by the State. There is an attempt to hush up the "Noes" and to gain a unanimous approval of the people who are wondering how we came to be involved in Korea. Do they know these facts about that country where we were "resisting aggression"? Absentee landlords owned most of the land in Korea, the largest being the Oriental Development Company, a Japanese-controlled corporation, which held title to more than half the farm land. Under Japanese rule, the smaller Korean farmers rapidly lost what land they owned, so that from 1918 to 1938 the number of tenant farmers increased by 45 percent. U.S. Department experts put the rent as high as 60 percent of the crop. Other sources put it as high as 90 percent. So little of the crop was left for the families that even in a good year they suffered hunger, the "spring hunger" during which they staved off starvation by living off bark and roots of trees, grass and earth. In rating the diet level of 70 countries, a recent pamphlet published by the United Nations Scientific and Cultural Commission put Korea at the bottom of the list with a per capita diet of only 1,904 calories a day.

"After U.S. troops took over from South Korea in 1945," George McCune wrote in his recent book, *Korea Today*, "the Oriental Development Company became the New Korea Company and an arm of the department of agriculture, and continued to operate not only its own varied interests, but in December, 1945, was designated as manager of all former Japanese-owned land. In 1947, U.S. financial journals estimated the assets of the corporation at $1,250,000,000 and stated that corporation controlled 64 percent of Korea's dry lands; 80 percent of its rice lands; 350,000 acres of forest lands. Its industrial holdings included shipbuilding, textiles, iron mining, alcohol, and shoe industries. The National City Bank of New York was its fiscal agent."

To repeat all these things is to run the risk of being accused of using Communist propaganda. The fact remains that in the Old Law, during a year of jubilee, lands that were mortgaged were returned, debts remitted, bondsmen freed. This has been no such Holy Year. The *Commonweal* editorial does not call for the liberation, the saving of the peoples of the East. "We must, for the time being," it reads, "leave the continent of Asia to its fate." It is now necessary, the article continues, "to save our own lives, our own way of life," so we must arm and hold Western Europe. In another part of the same issue there is a severe rebuke handed by one correspondent to Etienne Gilson for spreading a gospel of defeatism.

~

We shall of course be called defeatists and appeasers. Nevertheless I would say that our way of life, as we are living it, is not worth saving. Let us lay down our way of life, our life itself, rather than go on with this senseless slaughter.

It is possible to begin now to truly liberate our brother and ourselves, by beginning to fulfil the vows we made at our baptism, to renounce, in order to *be*—to put on Christ, Who laid down His life for His friends.

And not to speak in too general terms, to consider such steps as not paying income taxes, and whatever other forms of civil disobedience may prove effective, giving up jobs which contribute to the social disorder which makes for war; in other words, giving all things as Saint Matthew did and not going back to the tax office or money tables. Saint Peter could go back to his nets but not Saint Matthew to his money changing!

This is a call to the rich and the poor, and the great middle class of our country, in whose spiritual capacities I have faith. They are there, these great reserves of desire, at least, to help and love our brothers. And if we do not have the knowledge and courage to act, and if we lack leadership to inspire and guide us, God will bring it about that we will be stripped, to walk in His little way.

# The Story of Steve Hergenhan     **29**

STEVE HERGENHAN came to *The Catholic Worker* from Union Square. He was a German carpenter, a skilled workman who after forty years of frugal living had bought himself a plot of ground near Suffern, New York, and had proceeded to build on it, using much of the natural rock in the neighborhood. He built his house on a hillside and used to ski down to the village to get groceries. He did not like cars and would not have one. He thought that cars were driving people to their ruin. Workers bought cars who should buy homes, he said, and they willingly sold themselves into slavery and indebtedness for the sake of the bright new shining cars that speeded along the super highways. Maybe he refused to pay taxes for the roads that accommodated the cars. Maybe he was unable to. At any rate, he lost his little house on the side of the hill and ended up in New York, on a park bench during the day, telling his grievances to all who would listen, and eating and sleeping in the Municipal Lodging House, which then maintained the largest dormitory in the world, seven hundred double-decker beds.

Both Peter Maurin and Steve were agreed on a philosophy of work and the evils of the machine—they followed the writings of the distributists of England and the Southern agrarians in this country. But Steve differed from Peter on works of mercy. He declaimed loudly with Saint Paul, "He who does not work, neither let him eat." And no physical

Originally published in *Commonweal,* January 11, 1952. Vol. LV, 352–5.

or mental disability won his pity. Men were either workers or shirkers. It was the conflict between the worker and scholar that Peter was always talking about. Steve considered himself both a worker and a scholar.

When Hergenhan came to us, Peter begged him to consent to be used as a foil. Steve was to present the position of the Fascist, the totalitarian, and Peter was to refute him. They discoursed at our nightly meetings, in Union Square and Columbus Circle, and in Harlem, where we had been given the use of another store for the winter. They were invited to speak by Father Scully at a Holy Name meeting, and a gathering of the Knights of Columbus. How they loved these audiences in the simplicity of their hearts. Steve the German, Peter the Frenchman, both with strong accents, with oratory, with facial gesture, with striking pose, put on a show, and when they evoked laughter, they laughed too, delighted at amusing their audience, hoping to arouse them. "I am trying to make the encyclicals click," Peter used to say joyfully, radiant always before an audience. They never felt that they were laughed at. They thought they were being laughed with. Or perhaps they pretended not to see. They were men of poverty, of hard work, of Europe and America; they were men of vision; and they were men, too, with the simplicity of children.

But Hergenhan had bitterness too. The articles he wrote for *The Catholic Worker* about life in the Municipal Lodging House and the quest for bread of the homeless were biting. After the first one appeared, one of the city officials drove up with some companions in a big car and with unctuous flattery praised the work we were doing and asked us why we did not come to them first rather than print such articles about the work of the city.

"I tried to tell you," Hergenhan said. "I tried to tell you of the graft, the poor food, the treatment we received, the contempt and kicking around we got. But you threatened me with the psychopathic ward. You treated me like a wild beast. You gave me the bum's rush."

～

We rented a twelve-room house with a big attic, in Huguenot, Staten Island, right on the water, and there Steve planted a garden which was a model to all who came to participate in weekend conferences. Groups of young people came and speakers from Columbia University, from the Catholic University, from colleges in the Midwest, for these retreats and colloquiums.

They all talked, and Steve talked with the best of them, but they were young and he was past fifty; they were young students, second- or third-generation Italian, German, French, Irish, and Peter and Steve were first-generation. They listened to Peter because he never turned on them. Steve hated their avoidance of work, and after a good deal of recrimination turned from them to cultivate his garden.

The young fellows picketed the German consulate in protest against Nazism; they gave out literature at the docking of the *Bremen* and became involved in a riot when some Communists who called themselves Catholic workers tore down the swastika from the ship and were arrested. But Hergenhan just vented his scorn on youth in general and brought in great baskets of Swiss chard, tomatoes, beans and squash for us to admire and eat. It choked him to see the young people eat them. He wanted disciples who would listen to him and work with him.

The next year we received a letter from a Baltimore schoolteacher who wished to invest in a community. She offered us a thousand dollars provided we would build her a house and deed her three acres of the farm near Easton, Pennsylvania, to be purchased with her down payment. She would provide secondhand materials for the house.

We tried to dissuade her from coming to us, telling her of or dissensions, warning her she would be disappointed, but she insisted on contributing the money. She was disappointed of course, but when she sold her little house some ten years later, she got out of it a great deal more than she put into it. That didn't prevent her from writing to the Archbishop of Baltimore telling him that she had been lured to contribute to our farming commune by promises of community, which promises had proved false.

Steve always insisted that he had built her house single-handed. But Peter, and John and Paul Cort helped clean secondhand brick, pull nails out of the secondhand lumber, cart water up the hill from the spring and cisterns and dig the cellar, and there were many others who contributed many man-hours of labor. Of course much discussion went on with the building and digging. Hergenhan lived in a little shanty on the edge of the woods and came down to the farmhouse for his meals. He worked with great satisfaction on the house for two years. He was starting off the Catholic Workers with their first farming commune. He was showing them how to work, how to build, and he had great satisfaction in his toil. It was a spot of unutterable beauty looking down over the Delaware and the cultivated fields of New Jersey. Two and a half miles away at the foot of the hills were the twin cities of Easton and Philipsburg, one on either side of the river. Easton is a railroad center and a place of small factories, an old town with many historic buildings, and a college town, with Lafayette College perched upon a hill. There were Syrian, Lithuanian, German, Italian and Irish churches, and we had all these nationalities among us too.

~

Hergenhan built his house and then returned to the city to indoctrinate. He got tired of being considered the worker, and wanted to be a scholar for a time. But his bitterness had increased. In protest against our policies, specifically our works of mercy, he went to Camp La Guardia, a farm colony for homeless men run by the city. He wanted efficient and able-bodied workers building up village communities. We were clogged up with too much deadwood, with sluggish drones—it was the same old argument again, only this time it was a true worker and not just a young intellectual who was arguing the point.

He became ill and returned to us at Mott Street. We were his family after all. He was by then fifty-six. When he was examined the doctors discovered cancer, and after an operation he was taken to St. Rose's Cancer Hospital on the East Side, to die.

"Abandon hope all ye who enter here," he cried out when I came to visit him. He had not known of his cancer—they had talked of an intestinal obstruction at the hospital where the operation was performed—and when he was brought to St. Rose's he saw written over the door, Home of the Cancerous Poor.

His was a little room on the first floor; all day one could look into the garden and past that to the river where tugs and tankers steamed up and down the tidal river and clouds floated over the low shore of Brooklyn. The world was beautiful and he did not want to die. There was so much work he wanted to do, so small a part he had been allowed to play.

Peter and I used to go to see him every day. By that time I had just made what came to be known as our retreat and was filled with enthusiasm and ready to talk to anyone who would listen on the implications of the Christian life—and Steve always loved to converse, provided one gave him a chance to get in his share of the conversation.

I went to St. Rose's each day with my notes, and read them to him. He gradually became happy and reconciled. He had said, "There is so much I wanted to do." And I told him how Father John Hugo had talked of work, "that physical work was hard, mental work harder, and spiritual work was the hardest of all." And I pointed out that he was now doing the spiritual work of his life, lying there suffering, enduring, sowing all his own desires, in order to reap them in heaven. He began to realize that he had to die in order to live, that the door would open, that there was a glorious vista before him, "that all things were his."

I read Bede Jarrett's *No Abiding City* to him, and some of Father Faber's conferences on death, and he enjoyed them all. They offered him the richness of thought that he craved, and when the Sister who cared for him asked him if he did not want Baptism, he shouted wholeheartedly, "Yes!"

Peter and I were his sponsors, and to me it was a miracle of God's grace that the lack of dignity with which the Sacrament was conferred did not affront Steve, who was always hypercritical. He was baptized with speed and his confession listened to. He received Viaticum. I remember his anointing most vividly. Three other men were lined up on the bed at the same time, sitting there like gaunt old crows, their simple solemn faces lifted expectantly, childlike, watching every move of the priest, as he anointed their eyes, nose, mouth, ears, their clawlike hands stretched out to receive the holy oil, their feet with horny toes to which the priest bent with swift indifference.

$\sim$

Steve was baptized and anointed but he did not rally. Daily he became weaker and weaker and sometimes when I came I found him groaning with pain. Earlier at Roosevelt Hospital they had given him a brown-paper bag to blow into when he had an attack of pain. He would go through this ridiculous gesture as though he were going to break the bag explosively, as children do, but it was a desperate device like a woman's pulling on a roped sheet attached to the foot of the bed in the agonies of childbirth. Perhaps the intensities of pain and the intensity of pleasure are both somehow shameful because we so lose control, so lose ourselves, that we are no longer creatures of free will, but in the control of our blind flesh. "Who will deliver me from the body of this death?"

Steve died suddenly one morning, and there was no one with him. We found in his papers afterward notations which indicated his bitterness at not being more used, as writer, speaker, teacher. That has been the lament of so many who have died with us. Just as they are beginning to open their eyes to the glory and the potenialities of life their life is cut short as a weaver's thread. They were like the grass of the field. "The spaces of this life, set over against eternity, are most brief and poor," one of the desert fathers said. It is part of the long loneliness.

# Priest of the Immediate ............ 30

W E NOW HAVE the words of Abbé Pierre in print, but he himself did not write a book. *The Rag Pickers of Emmaus*, which Kenedy published early last year, was written by someone else, and *Abbé Pierre Speaks*, which was published last month by Sheed and Ward, is a collection of his talks. There was a tape recorder or a very good stenographer catching everything he said in sermons and over the radio, or in the intimacy of his own group, and the result is that you cannot read this book without feeling its immediacy and being stirred to the marrow of your bones. Here is a man of compassion, a priest of great heart who holds out his arms to all suffering ones. "Out of the fullness of the heart, the mouth speaketh," and thanks to all these translated notes, we know what is in Abbé Pierre's heart.

It was customary in an earlier age for priests to wander around Europe, as St. Francis did, as St. Ignatius and his band of twelve priests and laymen did, but we don't hear much of such adventures these days. There is not only more organization in the Church, there is more discipline. But World War II brought about many changes in Europe, and one of those changes meant great freedom in the life of many of France's priests. They still are conscripted, serve in the armies; ordained priests go to the front not only as chaplains but also as soldiers. Only last week a Sulpician told me that the seminaries in France were half

Originally published in *Commonweal*, December 28, 1956. Vol. LXV, 331–3.

empty because of the war in Africa. And after France was occupied and many of the priests taken prisoner, we had such accounts as Father Perrin's *Priest Workman in Germany,* the story of the priest in factory and in prison.

Abbé Pierre was one of these priests who "was hunted like a bandit for two years" when he served as a *maqui.* He was two years a chaplain in the navy and he also served in Africa. He was ordained a Capuchin but left the order to work as a parish priest. Later he served in the Chamber of Deputies in Paris, and it was thanks to his salary as a Deputy that he was able to start his first hospice, or rather very informally take in some of the needy men he encountered in the slums in Paris.

Besides being something of a politician, Abbé Pierre is something of an actor, wearing still, it would seem, the garb of chaplain, a beret, a string of service stripes and decorations across the front of his clerical garb, and regular clodhopper shoes. But if this makes him the more striking, if it calls attention to his role of prophet today, crying out for the poor, we may be only too happy that he has this flair, this streak of the romantic in him, to light up his role.

"You can live alongside people whose lives are horrible and absolutely hellish and not have the faintest idea of this because they have the decency and self-respect not to go shouting the fact from the roof top or whining about it in the streets. They are ashamed and degraded," he says.

He goes on to tell of a young man of twenty-five who came to tell him that his wife has just been taken away to a mental hospital. In the three years of their married life, they had been forced to share one room with two other families. He had two babies and another one on the way. The young man sat and wept like a child.

Another time he saw an eighteen-year-old girl who had been fished out of the Seine. She had been living with eleven other people in a hole dug for the foundations of a house which had never been finished, and in the winter rains had become a mudhole.

A priest in a neighboring parish called on him to come and try to help a family in his parish, living under a tarpaulin out in a field. They had been living there for eight months although the man was working. There simply was no housing for these poor workers. Two children had already died, and one little boy remained. Another child was on the way.

"It was then that I realized some terrible things," Abbé Pierre went on to say. "I realized that so long as people who were supposed to be apostles, as long as a priest like me was incapable of saying to that poor woman, 'Come on, get your things, pick up your child and come along with me and your husband and sleep in my room: I'll take your place in the tent and tomorrow we'll find some way of solving this,'—until then, well, fundamentally I was simply a humbug.

"In point of fact if I had talked to that poor woman, who had seen two of her children die, who was possibly expecting the one that was to be born to go the same way, and might even have been tempted to do away with it herself, if I had started talking to her about heaven and hell and the law of God, and told her that she had no right to do it, that it would be a crime—I was in the process of discovering that if I told her all that and then, having had my little say, left her in her tent in her field, to her misery and distress, whilst I, the priest, went back to my room, a poor room, no doubt, but even so a real room, where I could put an electric fire on when it turned cold, and could sleep peacefully in my bed, and be alone—if, after my little sermon, I failed to take her to some more cheerful place than her own, well, then, she was bound to think to herself, 'No doubt! It's all very fine what he says! Very true! But of course he is just a humbug like all the rest, for he's left me here in these dreadful conditions . . .'

"That's what I realized!

"Oh, we all ought to come to realize that! So long as we are incapable of behaving like Our Lord, that is to say, becoming incarnate, that is to say, going down and sharing the pain and suffering of the people we are supposed to be leading into the way of truth—well in point of fact we are simply humbugs."

~

It is well known, of course, what Abbé Pierre found to do. He had already gathered a crew of seventeen men. With his Deputy's salary and by their own work as ragpickers, these men somehow built shacks for one hundred and forty-one families. They put up tents; they bought land; they argued with the Minister of Reconstruction; they went out to the streets at night and with a truck full of bread, wine, soup and blankets tried to serve the destitute. Every night until three o'clock in the morning, Abbé Pierre was out with his rag-picking friends, gathering up those who were sleeping in the doorways, lying like bundles of rags near warm ventilators. They found one old woman dying on the pavement after being evicted from her room for nonpayment of rent.

A child died of cold and exposure. Abbé Pierre requested the Minister of Reconstruction to come to the funeral, and he did.

Then came his now-famous radio appeal on behalf of the homeless of Paris. In the broadcast he announced that he had set up two emergency stations, and he begged his listeners to bring what they could spare of blankets, food, funds. At the doors of the relief centers which were set up were the simple words:

> "Whoever you are, if you are suffering,
> Come in, sleep, eat and take heart.
> This is where you are loved."

And he begged his radio audience, "I beseech you, let us have enough love here and now to do this much! Let it be seen that so much suffering has at least given us back one wonderful thing: the soul of France!" And the people came with their gifts.

~

Yes, Abbé Pierre is a priest who sees the immediacy of the problem around him. Although he had been involved in political action, he recognized the need to do the immediate thing. He broke the law again and again, and because he had public opinion with him, and because all Paris could see the problem, he got away with it.

We visited with Abbé Pierre when he was in New York, and were happy to have him come to lunch at our house of hospitality. It was St. Joseph's day, and our house is called St. Joseph's house, so we always celebrate his feast. A butcher had given us enough chicken to feed the house, and the meal was a good one. It was lunch time, and in addition to the sixty people who live in the house there was a line of a few hundred men waiting outside. When Abbé Pierre arrived, scores of adulatory people came with him, and a dozen photographers, French and American. The place was a bedlam, but the house and the line enjoyed it mightily. Something was happening in their midst, and it was because of this man's love for them. When he left us he talked to the men on the line, and though he spoke in French he was understood, I know.

A branch of Abbé Pierre's "Companions of Emmaus" has been started in Montreal to build cooperative housing for the poor. We only wish that there were here in New York men with the ability to plan and build houses of hospitality for families instead of for single people as we have them now; to plan and build the farming communes which Peter Maurin, another Frenchman, a peasant, wrote and appealed for twenty-five years ago.

How Peter would have loved this other Peter! with his call for communities living in the midst of the poor, with their same poverty, begging for them, building for them. Abbé Pierre told how he stood before a vast basilica "for which they are collecting fantastic sums of money and how he cried out, 'Of course we need places of worship, but for mercy's sake, as long as you have slums in your town, as soon as you have built the four walls and put on a roof, stop decorating your sanctuary and understand this (and let us all understand it, for we all need to examine our consciences in this matter): it is not in the Eucharist that Jesus is cold; it is not in piling gold and marble and sumptuous stuffs round Jesus in the Eucharist that we shall honor Him; it is coming to His aid in the hands and feet of children throughout the world who are dying of cold and hunger because we have no care for them."

While I read this book and wrote these pages, I read too in the pages of a diocesan paper of a new convent being built to house sixteen nuns which was going to cost $85,000 and of a new foundling hospital for infants and children which was to cost ten million. Meanwhile, Mary Lisi lives around the corner on First Street in a cold little hole which costs her twelve dollars a week, and next to her are two more families paying even more rent for one room. Today our tenements are more congested than ever as they pull down more of the old.

It is time again to read the 25th Chapter of St. Matthew and to realize that it is by our treatment of the poor that we will be judged; and to pray for more priests of the vision and courage of Abbé Pierre, who realizes, as almost no one else seems to, that the family is the unit of society, and we must begin there.

# We Plead Guilty

# 31

---

*"We were, frankly, hoping for jail. Perhaps jail, we thought, would put another compulsion on us, of being more truly poor."*

---

THE MOST IMPORTANT contribution to thought made by the Catholic Worker, John Cort once said, was our emphasis on voluntary poverty. Whenever I am invited to speak at schools around the country and talk about the problems of destitution in this rich country, and in the name of the Catholic Worker receive praise, I feel guilty. When our readers and listeners say that I make them feel guilty, I can only say I feel more guilty. We live in the midst of destitution in a rich country, and when we sit down to eat, we know that there is a line waiting at the door so long that the house could not hold them. When we pass men lying on the streets at night, and see men huddled around a fire built against the old theater building next door, and we go into our St. Joseph's house of hospitality, into a house where men are sleeping on the floor (because all the beds are taken) and we go to our own warm and comfortable bed, once again we cannot help but feel guilty.

It is hard to comfort ourselves with the reflection that if we did not get rest and food we would not be able to do the work we do. We can reflect that some of the poverty we profess comes from lack of privacy, lack of time to ourselves. We can list instances of sights and sounds, smells and feelings that one can never get used to nor fail to cringe

Originally published in *Commonweal*, December 27, 1957. Vol. LXVII, 330–3.

from. Yet God has blessed us so abundantly, has provided for us so constantly over these twenty-five years that we are always in the paradoxical position of rejoicing and saying to ourselves "our lines are fallen in goodly places." "It is good, Lord, to be here." We feel overwhelmed with graces, and yet we know we fail to correspond to them. We fail far more than seven times daily, failing in our vocation of poverty especially. As we think of all this, our feeling of guilt persists.

For this reason, as well as for the reason that we are pacifists, we refused to take part in the war maneuvers, if you can call them that, of the compulsory civil defense drills of the past three years. We were, frankly, hoping for jail. Ammon Hennacy, one of our editors, frankly says he wants to be a martyr. And as for me, I feel of course that the servant is not above the master, that we must take up our cross and follow our Master. Perhaps jail, we thought, would put another compulsion on us, of being more truly poor. Then *we* would not be running a house of hospitality, *we* would not be dispensing food and clothing, *we* would not be ministering to the destitute, but would be truly one with them. We would be truly among the least of God's children, sharing with them their misery. Then we could truly say in the prayers at the foot of the altar, "poor banished, children of Eve, mourning and weeping in this valley of tears." How hard it is to say it, surrounded by material and spiritual benefits as we are!

And so on three occasions we have been imprisoned. Each time we have gone through the gruelling experience of torturous rides in the police van, sitting for long hours in prison cells awaiting booking or trial. In the first year, we had only an overnight experience of jail (which necessitated, however, the examinations for drugs, the humiliations of being stripped and showered and deprived of clothing and belongings). The second year the sentence was five days, and this last summer it was thirty days (with five days off for good behavior).

When we were locked in that first night in a narrow cell meant for one but holding two cots, we had just passed through an experience which was as ugly and horrifying as any I may ever experience. I know that St. Paul said, "Let these things not so much as be mentioned among you," and it is not as a litterateur I speak, but as a Christian, who shares the guilt of all. We had been processed, we clutched our wrappers around us, and as we got off the elevators on the seventh floor to be assigned our cells, we were surrounded by a group of young women, colored and white, Puerto Rican and American, who first surveyed us boldly and then started making ribald comments. Deane Mowrer and I were older women though Deane was younger than I, and Judith Beck was young and beautiful. She was an actress which means that she carries herself consciously, alert to the gaze of others, responding to it. Her black hair hung down around her shoulders, her face was very pale, but she had managed to get some lipstick on before the officers took all her things away from her.

"Put her in my cell," one of the roughest of the Puerto Rican girls shouted, clutching at Judith. "Let me have her," another one called out. It was a real hubbub, ugly and distracting, coming as it did on top of hours of contact with prison officials, officers, nurses and so on.

I had a great sinking of the heart, a great sense of terror for Judith. Was this what jail meant? We had not expected this type of assault—and on the part of women. With the idea of protecting Judith, I *demanded*, and I used that term too for the only time during my imprisonment, that she be put in my cell or Deane's cell if we had to be doubled up because of crowding. "I will make complaints," I said very firmly, "if you do not do this."

The jeering and controversy continued, but the officer took us to our respective cells, putting Judith and me in one, and Deane in another at the opposite corridor. Later, Joan Moses, a young Protestant demonstrator, who had gone alone with her husband to Times Square and made a public refusal to take shelter, and who was tried three days after we were, joined us, and she and Deane, and Judith and I, were put into adjoining cells.

~

We felt this sense of separation from the other prisoners, and as we were locked in that first night, I thought of a recent story by J. D. Salinger which I had read in the *New Yorker*, "Zooie." It is about the impact of the Prayer of Jesus, famous among pilgrims in Russia, on a young girl from an actor's family. The prayer is, "My Lord Jesus Christ, Son of the Living God, have mercy on me a sinner." Sometimes the prayer is shortened: "My Lord Jesus, have mercy on me a sinner." Sometimes it is accompanied by prostrations, sometimes by a way of breathing, "My Lord Jesus" being said as one inhales, and the rest of the prayer as one exhales. Eastern theologians warn against using this prayer without spiritual direction. Dr. Bulgakoff states that according to the theology of the Eastern Church, at the very mention of the Holy Name, there He is in the midst of us.

The girl Frannie in Salinger's story has become entangled in this prayer and is in such a state that her mother is about to get the advice of a psychiatrist. But the brother, who has been educated with his sister by an older brother who is something of a mystic, accomplishes her release from the hysteria into which she had plunged through a ceaseless repetition of the Jesus prayer, in a long conversation which makes the story more than a short story. He convinces her finally that she is trying to use a short cut to religious experience, that fundamentally she scorns others and is turning to God to escape from contact with humankind; and he reminds her of a piece of advice given her by an older brother. When she was acting in a radio play, as she had been the summer before, she was to remember the fat lady sitting on her porch rocking and listening to the radio. In other words, "Jesus Christ is the fat lady."

Part of the impact of the story is the contrast between the reverence (the Russians would have rejected "My Jesus, mercy!" as being too intimate) and, not only the last line, the punch line, but the irreverent language which leads up to it, the compulsive use of the Holy Name. The rest of its power lies in the profound Christian truth said over and over again by the saints, after our Lord Himself said it: He has left Himself in the midst of us, and what we can no longer do for Him we can do for them.

We were locked in our cells, and all the other five hundred women in the House of Detention were locked in theirs. The lights would go out at nine-thirty. The noise, the singing, the storytelling, the wildly vile language would go on until then. We were stunned by the impact of our reception, and the wild, manic spirits of all those young women about us. The week's work was finished, it was Friday night, and here were two days of leisure ahead.

I thought of this story of Salinger's and I found it hard to excuse myself for my own immediate harsh reaction. It is all very well to hate the sin and love the sinner in theory but it is hard to convey that idea in practice. By my peremptory rejection of the kind of welcome we received, I had of course protected Judith, but there was no expression of loving friendship in it towards the others. Lying there on my hard bed, I mourned to myself, "Jesus is the fat lady. Jesus is this unfortunate girl."

Jackie was released the next day; she had spent her six months, or her year or her two years, or whatever it was. One of the horrors of the House of Detention is that it is not just a place for the women awaiting trial as it was planned to be, but that it is used as a workhouse and penitentiary too, situated unsuitably though it is in the center of the city. A week later, we saw in the *Daily News,* which can be purchased by the inmates, that Jackie had attempted suicide and had been taken to Bellevue psychiatric prison ward. And a week after that she was back in the House of Detention, but on another floor.

⁓

The other prisoners certainly did not harbor any hostility to us nor take offense at the openness of my judgment. It was my interior fear and harshness that I was judging in myself. We had not been issued clothing, and the officers were not going to allow us to go to the chapel in our wrappers. So our kind fellow-prisoners, sensing our keen disappointment, gathered together clothing, underwear, socks and shoes and dresses, so that we could go to Mass and receive Communion. Prostitutes, drug addicts, forgers and thieves had more loving kindness toward us than our jailers, who had no sense of the practice of religion being a necessity to us, but acted as though it were a privilege which they could withhold.

Of all the five hundred women in the Women's House of Detention only about fifteen got to Mass. By being importunate, I got to see the priest, to ask that my Bible, missal and breviary be permitted me. He was most reserved, withdrawn, and I had the impression that besides being aloof with women in general, he was most especially aloof with women prisoners. The chaplain was a man who might have been able to show a little warmth and human kindness and sympathy, but in addition to the jail, he also tended St. Vincent's Hospital and St. Joseph's Church. So we could not see much of him. On that day we obtained a small pamphlet Mass book and a diocesan paper to read.

Later, on the window sill in the dining room, I came across a copy of an old *New Yorker,* and in it a poem by W. H. Auden. He had come to my rescue the year before when I had been convicted of being a slum landlord. At that time he brought me the money to pay my $250 fine, a sentence which was afterwards suspended. It was like a visit from a friend to find this poem of Auden's. There was a refrain, "Thousands have lived without love, but none without water." This may not be exact—I am quoting from memory—but I know Judith sang it as she rejoiced in the one truly sensual enjoyment of the day, the shower. It was ninety-five degrees outside, and our cell was most oppressive. We indeed felt that we could not live without water.

Within a few days we were able to go to the library which is situated on the second floor of the House of Detention. It is a very good library and one can take out five books a week. Not that there is time to read five books, what with the work schedule each day. I borrowed *Resurrection,* by Tolstoy, that great story of a trek to Siberia of a concourse of prisoners, the royalties from which were donated by Tolstoy to pay for the emigration of the Doukhobors to Canada to escape the persecution they were undergoing in Russia for their pacifism. I had read the work before and had been especially impressed by the picture of the separation of the political prisoners and the ordinary criminals in the line. There was no such separation in our case.

I read *Northanger Abbey* by Jane Austen and was charmed by her defense of the novel form. I read *Embezzled Heaven* and travelled on pilgrimage with the old servant woman. *Kon Tiki* was a joy indeed and one could feel the spray of the open ocean on one's face and wonder at the great daring of these modern explorers. I was rather afraid to read Mann's *Doctor Faustus,* which my cell mate had taken out of the library—there was already enough emphasis on evil everywhere—but was happy to have my attention called to the beautiful descriptions of music which are in it.

The most startling thing I read in jail was a series of essays, entitled *Lenin,* by Trotsky, published back in 1926 or thereabouts. How had this book found its way into the library of one our city prisons? But I read it with interest. Trotsky described the moments he spent with Lenin when the revolution had become an accomplished fact, and Kerensky was driven out and Lenin and Trotsky had become the acknowledged leaders. "Lenin made the sign of the cross before his face," Trotsky wrote.

$\sim$

But it was remembering Salinger, and Dostoevsky's Father Zossima, and Alyosha and the Honest Thief, and reading Tolstoy's short stories, that made me feel that again we had failed. We had the luxury of books—our horizons were widened though we were imprisoned. We could not certainly consider ourselves poor. Each day I read the prayers and the lessons from my daily missal and breviary to Judith, and when I told her stories of the fathers of the desert, she told me tales of the Hassidim. On the feast of St. Mary Magdalene I read:

"On my bed at night I sought him
Whom my heart loves—
I sought him but I did not find him.

I will rise then and go about the city;
 in the streets and crossings I will seek
Him whom my heart loves.
I sought him but I did not find him . . .

Oh, that you were my brother,
 nursed at my mother's breasts!
If I met you out of doors, I would kiss you
 and none would taunt me.
I would lead you, bring you in
 to the home of my mother. . . .

Rejoice with me, all you who love the Lord, for
I sought him and he appeared to me. And while I
 was weeping at the tomb, I saw my Lord,
 Alleluia.

Yes, we fail in love, we make our judgments and we fail to see that we are all brothers, we all are seeking love, seeking God, seeking the beatific vision. All sin is a perversion, a turning from God and a turning to creatures.

If only our love had been stronger and truer, casting out fear, I would not have taken a stand, I would have seen Christ in Jackie. Suppose Judith had been her cell mate for the night and had been able to convey a little of the love the pacifists feel is the force which will overcome war. Perhaps, perhaps. . . . But this is the kind of analyzing and introspection and examination of conscience the narrator in *The Fall* indulged in after he heard that cry in the dark, that splash in the Seine and went his way without having helped his brother, only to hear a mocking laughter that followed him ever after.

Thank God for retroactive prayer! St. Paul said that he did not judge himself, nor must we. We can turn to our Lord Jesus Christ who has repaired already the greatest evil that ever happened or could ever happen, and trust that He will make up for our falls, for our neglects, for our failures in love.

# Letter: From Dorothy Day

# 32

TO THE EDITORS: It was brought to my attention only the other day that Monsignor McCaffrey, chaplain to the women at the House of Detention in Greenwich Village, was very much hurt by my reference to him as not interested in the women under his care ["We Plead Guilty," Dec. 27, 1957]. I have written him a most belated letter of apology, but also explained, passing some of the blame on to you, that there were a few sentences deleted in my manuscript which changed the sense of that paragraph. If you will please print this letter, it may clear up his hurt, although I'm afraid it may hurt another priest!

I said that Monsignor McCaffrey had the care not only of the women but also of the St. Vincent's Hospital, besides his own parish, and that on that first Sunday morning, it was a young priest who offered Mass, who showed no interest in the women, but walked in looking neither to the right or left and that I had a hard time getting a few words to him, begging for a visit from Monsignor McCaffrey, the chaplain. The message was conveyed, and Monsignor McCaffrey came to visit me, and was most kind, bringing me a Missal and magazines to read. I do not think that much more than a sentence was deleted from my original article, but it was enough to make it appear that it was Monsignor McCaffrey who was not interested in the women. When I finally got around to reading over the printed article, I was upset at the implication, but then it slipped my mind and I did nothing to rectify it.

Originally published in *Commonweal*, June 13, 1958. Vol. LXVIII, 282–3.

Now the matter has been brought to my attention, at this late date. I have written to the Monsignor to apologize and I would be grateful if you would also print this public apology.

As for the "young priest" I spoke of. It is a hard assignment, to come into a prison of five hundred women, and one needs special interest and the special grace to do the work. Not every priest is suited for it. It is not especially the age of the priest. I can see a young Father Hessler, the missioner, speaking with fervor, and loving kindness and warmth to the prisoners, telling them the lives of the saints, giving them some vision of a life other than their own, trying to awaken in them longings and desires for the love of God and for a life of grace. I am praying for such chaplains for women prisoners at the House of Detention.

Do print this letter soon. It will serve to remind your readers to pray for us all, and for all prisoners, all over the world. It is a forgotten work of mercy.

# Pilgrimage to Mexico

# 33

I SPENT SIX MONTHS in Mexico back in 1929, most of the time in Mexico City and Xochimilco. The churches had just been reopened and there was only one priest in all the capital who heard confessions in English. His understanding of the language was so bad he shouted to make you understand *him,* and the other penitents kept tactfully the church-length away during the long afternoon's wait to be heard. The political situation was bad, but when isn't it? It was a time of fiesta days, and every time the fireworks exploded we thought another revolution was starting.

Diego Rivera was among the many Mexicans I met then. He was large and genial and had just come back from Russia, where, he told me, I had rubles waiting for me for the many translations into all the languages of the U.S.S.R. of my article "Having a Baby," which had originally appeared in *The Masses.* It was a happy article and I was glad to hear that it had been translated. The baby, then going on four years old, was with me there. She had been baptized four months after birth and I had been baptized eighteen months later.

I remember Rivera well, and I remember that I had been up against enough anti-Catholic and anti-religious propaganda among some of the artists and writers of *The Masses* not to be shocked at his attitude toward religion. I probably even agreed with much of Rivera's criticism, especially in regard to the wealth of the Church and the luxury of

Originally published in *Commonweal,* December 26, 1958. Vol. LXIX, 336–8.

the clergy. But my Catholicism was an act of faith. "Though he may slay me, yet will I trust in Him." It had seemed like death, at the time, to become a Catholic.

The serious articles which I wrote while in Mexico about the political situation, were all rejected by the Catholic magazines to which I submitted them. So I remembered the journalistic training I had received under Lionel Moise, the famed city editor who also taught journalism to Ernest Hemingway, and I began writing features about Tamar and myself. It was the beginning of Tamar's life in print and she has had to be content to be a part of my writing ever since. (Once when there was a long gap in my mention of her in articles a reader wrote to ask if she were dead!) I wrote about our visit to Our Lady of Guadalupe's shrine, about Easter in Xochimilco, about living with a Mexican family, about Adolpho Fuentes of the revolutionary party who took us on picnics in his truck on Sundays, about living with the people (Communists would call them the peasants) who farmed the man-made islands of Xochimilco.

I was there six months at that time and only returned to New York because Tamar became ill. And now I have spent another two weeks on a pilgrimage there. I presume to write about Mexico on the basis of just this much experience, but then Evelyn Waugh wrote an entire book about Mexico after only a two months' visit. He did not apologize, saying that it is the function of the journalist to "hope to notice things which the better experienced accept as commonplace and to convey to a distant public some idea of the aspect and feel of a place."

~

The two articles I wrote in *The Catholic Worker* about this pilgrimage called forth some sharp rebukes from critics of the Church who blame all the poverty and illiteracy of Mexico on the clergy. Who is their scapegoat for the poverty I have seen in America, that of the sharecroppers and the tenant farmers, the migrant workers, the Negroes and Puerto Ricans in our city slums? And why has not the revolution done more for the poor in Mexico in the hundred years since the reform laws were passed? But I do not want to enter into controversy. I will get on with my impressions, because that is all this article will be.

"But did you enjoy yourself?" Fritz Eichenberg asked me, after he had read my two articles in *The Catholic Worker,* and since they were apparently not personal enough for him, I shall make this very personal.

Yes, it was a happy trip. I enjoyed Father Neudecker's talk on the train between Kansas City and San Antonio and Laredo (and that part of the trip was most comfortable). I enjoyed the cartons of good whole wheat bread which he had baked himself at Kellogg, Minnesota, where he "earns his living" by grinding wheat and selling good flour as St. Paul earned his by sailmaking. I enjoyed his sitting up with us all night on the trip from the border to San Luis Potosi (accent on the last syllable), when it was freezing cold and the doors of the car would not stay closed. The old missionary with us took a berth, thank God, and the other priest, who should have, caught a very bad cold, but maybe it was Father Neudecker's whole wheat bread which saved him. The toilets over-flowed, the car became filthy, but still it was not as bad as the front cars, which were of wood, with wooden seats and open windows.

Yes, I enjoyed that cold night—it was part of a pilgrimage. I enjoyed it as St. Francis did the ashes on his bread. Coming into San Luis Potosi four hours late, we received Communion at one of the three Masses offered, and then had our first solid meal at a little hotel. (Of course we had had plenty of Father Neudecker's bread.) Then our three guides drove us in their three cars over the most beautiful mountains and plains to Guanajuante, a town so entrancing that I should choose to stay there rather than at Taxco or Cuernavaca or any other tourist place. We put up for two nights at the Sante Fe hotel on the plaza. At night a band played and the boys and girls walked around and around, the boys going in one direction and the girls in another so that they were constantly repassing one another. When the band stopped, other musicians with stringed instruments and very solemn faces played Mexican music and sang mournfully.

~

The next morning after an early Mass we set out for the Mountain of Christ the King, on the top of which is a great shrine, a tremendous statue like that of our Statue of Liberty, which was erected on this highest mountain of central Mexico to replace one which had been bombed by a lone Communist aviator back in 1928 or before. Perpetual adoration is offered at a shrine of the Benedictine nuns of Christ the King in a convent a little way down the mountain, which is seven thousand feet high. You can imagine the view of the world around us in that crystal clear air, high, high above the surrounding hills and plains.

One of the things about this old civilization is that no matter how far you go in the wilderness there are always signs of human habitation. There are no fences, but there are always shepherds and herdsmen, on foot, living with their animals, father and son, sitting with neighbor father and son. Oxen do the ploughing, harvesting is by hand, threshing is as it was in Biblical times. The land is old, and the ways of the people are ancient, too. They are lean and spare and pruned to the bone.

The next day we started promptly at nine o'clock in the morning and drove in our three cars to San Miguel d'Allende, named not only for St. Michael but also for d'Allende, a national hero who (as one of the guides told us) pushed Father Hidalgo into revolution when he hesitated. We had an elaborate lunch there, in a hotel which was formerly a Franciscan monastery and is now the most luxurious building the town offers for travelers' accommodations, and visited the art school, which is also a former monastery. It is not only that the Orders were robbed of their possessions and of the fruit of their hard work; there is evidence too of a decline in vocations and the ability to build such foundations again.

We drove another hundred miles to Tolucca, and then on for forty-five miles to Mexico City. The city was a dazzling sight, a sea of jewels, as we came down the mountains into the old lake bed where the city is situated. Our hotel was spacious, with hot baths and high ceilings, but it was on a mean, narrow street. There was no restaurant in the hotel nor any near at hand, and the other pilgrims wanted to move, which we did the next day, although it was Sunday.

It is strange about pilgrimages. The high point should have been that Sunday morning, when we went out to the shrine of Our Lady of Guadalupe, three miles away from the center of the city. Street cars and buses, cabs, taxis, every kind of conveyance was directed toward that little hill of Tepayac, where the Blessed Mother, in the guise of a young Indian maiden of fifteen, appeared to Juan Diego (the Spanish name for the Indian) and told him that she would be the protectress of the Indians, that she loved them. Everyone knows the story, how she filled his tilma, a sort of burlap blanket he wore over his shoulders, with Castilian roses, which did not grow in that part of the country or at that time of year at all. He brought his roses to the Bishop, who, with those around him, at once fell on his knees in veneration. For there on the tilma was painted a miraculous picture of the Indian Aztec Virgin, Our Lady of Guadalupe. This all happened in 1531, and the best telling of it, from the original documents, is to be found in *The Dark Virgin* by Donald Demarest.

But the moment of exaltation does not come according to a time-table. We were on pilgrimage, and we had guides who had scheduled our tour—one day we were to be here, another there. Very often, of course, we did slip away from each other and kneel in those magnificent churches and basilicas among the people of Mexico City and among the poor, barefoot, white-clad, silent and devout, who kneel for hours, their arms outstretched, their eyes on the face of the Virgin or our Crucified Lord. It was all so different from everything we knew, that we had been accustomed to. We were distracted constantly by the crowds, and by the individuals who absorbed our attention. And there was the climate, the rarefied air at that tremendous altitude, twelve thousand feet.

~

A pilgrimage like this is the time to be carried along with the others, to keep a diary, or to write letters home that will be saved for you to refresh your memory with. Later on, it is often a sudden smell of charcoal or beeswax, or the feel of cold stone under your knees, or the sight of another at worship that recalls you.

I visited the shrine again before we left, but I am always terribly distracted by people. No matter how long I stay, no matter how resolutely I try to close my eyes, ears and thought, my worship remains an act of will, a gesture of the body. I am present, but I am not carried away. Certainly I am more often overtaken by joy and thanksgiving in my own parish church at home. No matter how much of a pilgrim I consider myself, and call myself, I am wedded to home, to the house of hospitality, to the parish where we live in New York. It is my vocation.

On our last day we had an audience with Archbishop Miranda, and he kept us for two hours, talking to us about the Church in Mexico. We felt blessed indeed. The laws against the Church are still on the books, as they are in France, he pointed out. It is not only in Russia that the Church is being persecuted. The great need, he said, is for vocations, and for lay apostles to help the priests. This great archbishop is also a believer in nonviolent resistance to oppression. During the worst of the persecution there was not a bishop in Mexico who advocated armed resistance. Always the emphasis was on the spiritual weapons, on prayer and suffering. There were many martyrs.

Sunday, after Mass, I left on the noon bus, the Chuihuahua line, for El Paso, the ticket costing eleven dollars and fifty cents. The other pilgrims were returning by train or plane. The roads were good, the seats conducive to relaxed comfort, we were warm though there was a severe cold spell through central Mexico and I was overjoyed to hear one of my fellow passengers reading aloud, from a copy of *The Catholic Worker* which I had given her. She was reading some of Peter Maurin's *Easy Essays* to the only other English-speaking passenger in the crowded bus. Not at all distracted by the hubbub around her, she read and laughed aloud, and constantly said, "But this is remarkable!"

Peter Maurin, Catholic Worker founder, had reached a few more people, and I was on my way home, back to work with the new strength one always gains from a pilgrimage.

# In Memory of Ed Willock     34

A FTER PETER MAURIN died, a group of people who had known him sat down and wrote short essays about what Peter had meant to them, and these were published in pamphlet form by the Pio Decimo Press in Monsignor Hellriegel's parish in St. Louis. We have been grateful ever since for that small pamphlet.

And now that Ed Willock is dead I think that many of us who knew him in the past should write a bit of what he meant to us, of what we knew of him. Arthur Sheehan who met him first in Boston made a beginning in the January issue of *The Catholic Worker*.

In the same issue of the paper we reprinted two essays of Willock's which were direct and forthright criticisms of positions of laity and clergy of the present day; coming as they did right after the Bishops' recent statement on Personal Responsibility, they were particularly pertinent. These essays were reprints—nothing he had written recently. He had not been able to write much in recent years, but there were some good articles that Bishop Waters used in his diocesan paper and tried to get syndicated so that Ed could earn a living as he had in the past.

These later articles were on the family, and since Ed and Dorothy were parents of twelve children, it would be thought that they had a right to speak. But Ed said wryly (while he was still able to talk) that there were so many priests writing about the family that there was not much room for the laity to voice their ideas.

Originally published in *Commonweal*, February 24, 1961. Vol. LXXIII, 549–51.

Of course priests come from families too.

But I will begin at the beginning. I met Ed first at our Boston house of hospitality where he had done some beautiful murals for the walls. I thought of him always as a painter, an artist, a cartoonist, and I knew that he had earned a living sometimes painting billboards—not the first good artist to have done this kind of work, certainly.

These were depression years; talking about it afterwards to me, Ed said that the greatest disgrace a New Englander felt was to be without work, without a job with which to support a family. Like many another young man, he left home on that account, and came to the house of hospitality on Tremont Street in Boston, right off the Common, and worked with the Boston group there.

People made speeches on the Common and people listened to them. (That was why Peter Maurin loved Boston, because it had a Common, a bit of common land.) Ed met Peter there and they had many an Easy Conversation, as Peter called them.

Ed always said that he learned many things from Peter. "There can be no revolution without a theory of revolution," Peter quoted Lenin as saying and Ed listened to Peter work out a theory of the Green Revolution. Peter's theory hit the high spots, as he leaped from crag to crag in his lofty thought. Ed wanted to fill in the spaces, to make the way plain.

~

Peter thought in terms of the apostolate, the single man and woman, the workers and scholars on a farming commune. Ed Willock thought in terms of family and community. And always of man's work, the breath of life to him, more important than food, that aspect of his life that makes him most like God, in Whose image and likeness he was created, man the co-creator with God, like God in that he too is a creator.

There were many marriages in the Catholic Worker movement always because when young people start working together, it is a more real courtship than just going together, going steady. When the Boston group together with readers from the Worcester, Massachusetts, area started a house of hospitality in Worcester, young college girls came to help, and the girl who became Dorothy Willock was one of them.

In all the busyness of the Catholic Worker movement during those years, I lost track of the Willocks until I began encountering Ed's work as both writer and artist in the *Torch*, the Dominican magazine published in New York of which Father Wendell is the editor. Carol Jackson, a convert, was also writing for the *Torch* and had the same ideas as Ed did. It was her idea I think that made them start the magazine *Integrity,* which was to run for many years and prove to be such a source of inspiration to so many students and intellectuals.

Ed and Carol printed in its entirety Cardinal Suhard's inspiring articles, *Growth or Decline,* and *Priests Among Men* which we used for discussions held for a week at a time at our Maryfarm retreat house. There were entire issues on Marriage, on the Family, on Community, and Ed wrote of life and of death with courage and dignity.

Many new writers were introduced to *Integrity* readers, and Ed's articles, clearly reasoned, logical, profoundly Catholic, showed the Dominican influence on his thought. He was himself a third order Dominican, and when he died he was buried in a habit Father Wendell brought.

The magazine *Integrity* became so popular that young people flocked to it and visitors came from all over the country to sit around the office and discuss the ideas in the last month's or the future month's articles. Ed himself had to fix up a room in the basement where he could hide out if he wished to get any work done.

He was invited to speak everywhere, of course. He had a growing family but he never set any fees. He spoke at the C.W. as willingly as he spoke at some school where he would be paid. And it was from one of these meetings that Marycrest, at Orangeburg, New York, grew. A piece of land was chosen because it was within commuting distance of New York, and as soon as the land was purchased, a group of men headed by Ed started to help each other build homes.

~

Ed Willock worked tirelessly in that community, and went on with his speaking, writing and editing outside of it. His house, as some of the others, went up bit by bit. They are the kind of houses perhaps that would never be finished, what with growing families. Ed needed more room than others did, with the increasing children, and yet when they had the money to put a second story on the house it had to be used for another kind of sewage system, or an improvement in the roadway. I do not know what taxes they paid, nor how the burden was shared.

All I know is that Ed worked harder than most men. And then one day we heard that he had been stricken and was partially paralyzed, that Dorothy had to be with him night and day those first weeks, and that it was not certain whether he would live or die. I do not know the exact nature of his illness, but it resulted in high blood pressure and repeated strokes.

The very day we heard this sad news, two young girls were coming to us from Minnesota to give us a year to help with the Catholic Worker house of hospitality and Peter Maurin Farm. One was a trained nurse and she went willingly and immediately to spend her year with the Willocks. That is the kind of devotion they inspired.

Later others went to help out as Ed got better or worse, and crisis succeeded crisis. A young poet and a young writer spent time there, trying to help take care of a wild young brood. Another young woman went into service, one might say, working for a wealthy woman as general housekeeper for sixty a week and her keep, and saved all the money to try again to get a second story put on the Willock house. A friend matched what she earned and another crisis was met.

Ed Willock was, in a way, a Job. He exemplified the mystery of human suffering. When I told the head of one of our groups, married and with children, he cried out at the tragedy of this but added, "What is going to happen to us? We must all suffer?" And his family too was stricken later on with a child afflicted with virus which left him deaf, dumb, blind and completely blank mentally.

The only way to explain it, of course, is the Fall. Without the doctrine of original sin, the evil in the world would be an unbearable mystery. "All nature itself travailleth and groaneth even until now," St. Paul said, and Juliana of Norwich said, to comfort us, as women are made to do, "The worst has already happened, but it has been repaired. All will be well, and all will be well, and all will be very well."

~

I speak so much of these mysteries, this need for man to fill up the sufferings of Christ, to bear with Christ the pain which will be His until the end of time, because this is how we all thought of it when we thought of Ed. It was not only his own little community around him, in which he was now a "useless" member (he never ceased to suffer over that) but it was a larger community, all over the country, who thought these thoughts.

I remember Father John J. Hugo saying once, at one of our retreats, that manual work was hard, and mental work was harder but that spiritual work was the hardest of all, and suffering is a great part of that spiritual work he spoke of. We all felt Ed was suffering for us all. If one looks at all men all over the world as members, or potential members, of the Mystical Body of Christ, Ed had been chosen among those worthy to suffer, to lighten the load for others, to take some of the suffering of families today upon himself, willing or unwilling though he might be.

"Let us suffer if needs be with bitterness," the Little Flower said, "but let us suffer." And Ed suffered with bitterness, to the end. He was doing the hardest work of all. He was using the weapons of the spirit in the warfare against principalities and powers.

It is all very well to talk of mounting the Cross joyfully, with Christ, singing. Suffering is not like that except perhaps for a woman bringing new life into the world. But Ed died daily. He was literally putting off the old man, and putting on Christ, as St. Paul said, "and there was no beauty in him."

He endured stroke after stroke. He was unable to speak and had to write on a slate half the time. Sometimes he could articulate more clearly, and Dorothy always seemed to know what he wanted to say. He had to be fed with a spoon, because much of the time he could not swallow. Dorothy had to do all this at the times when he was most ill. He wanted her with him always and there were the children. His mind was never affected, and so in that way he suffered the more.

There were times when he was better and he came to Newburgh, Maryfarm, for our retreats, or parts of them. Father Marion Casey went to him at Marycrest and talked to a group there. When we got the beach cottages, Dorothy brought him there, and I can see him yet sitting in a wicker chair looking out over the water and listening to the tides come in, breathing in the salt fresh air. He could not read for more than a few minutes at a time.

Two years ago he spent Thanksgiving at Peter Maurin Farm, and Michael, his oldest son, kept the fires going in the "priest's room" which had been made from a wagon shed, and waited on his father, and sometimes Ed could make himself understood and sometimes he had to take to writing on a slate. He could hear perfectly, of course, but it was sad to have to do so much of the talking when that brilliant mind had to confine itself to a few short sentences at a time.

We talked for a long time then, and I don't think there is a suffering Ed and his family endured that I do not know about. And it was complete, even to the cold disapprobation of those who asked, "What right did he have, to have so many children when he was not able to support them?" That was the cruelest blow of all, coming from his peers, and not all the help, the mutual aid of his greater family around the country could make up for it. "But God will wipe all tears from his eyes."

Let others write of the thought of Ed Willock; let all that he has written be reprinted and read by many. I can only write as a woman, and pray that Ed now knows what "eye hath not seen, nor ear heard, of all that God has prepared for those that love him."

Ed was a man who lived, and loved, and died, and all he wrote was tried as though by fire, in the crucible of life itself.

# Southern Pilgrimage

# 35

COMING UP from New Orleans to Baton Rouge—home of the Legislature which has five times fired the school board and appointed a new one, none of which has been accepted by the people—the highway is an ugly one, plastered with billboards and service stations and motels. Later on you come to a long, shaded road, shaded with live oaks, Spanish moss, a bayou on one side with turtles and cranes and yellow flowers among the patches of green along the water. But the town of Kenner, where Father Jerome Drolet lives, is still amidst the billboards. You turn to the left of them, go down a little main street and there, one block to the right, are the school, convent, rectory and white frame church. There is a lovely flower garden around the rectory, with sweet peas climbing up the wire fence, roses in bloom, yellow calendulas, and many other flowers.

Father Drolet had his picture on the first page of the *New York Times* in December, for joining in protest with a Methodist minister who went out to preach the gospel to the creatures who made up a screaming mob to persecute the colored parents escorting their children to the two integrated schools in New Orleans. Father Drolet, who is the pastor of his church, is a tall, good-looking man with a deeply lined face, still young. I first met him in 1937 during the seamen's strike, when he went around the waterfront collecting aid for the striking seamen in the strike which led to the formation of the National Maritime Union. He

Originally published in *Commonweal*, March 31, 1961. Vol. LXXIV, 10–12.

visited them in prison and in hospitals. "Blessed is he who remembers the needy and the poor," and they certainly were poor and persecuted that winter of the big strike.

Originally from Illinois, Father Drolet came to Louisiana and went through the seminary and was ordained priest to preach the gospel to the poor. Knowing that the gospel cannot be preached to men with empty stomachs, he turned to the works of mercy. But pastors often complain of the zeal of young curates, and Father Drolet found himself in Houma, Louisiana, among the sugar cane workers and shrimp fishers and cannery workers. (The minimum wage there is still fifty-eight cents an hour, he says.) Then he started a house of hospitality in a store front, opened up an integrated ball park and playground for the children, took in the wayfarer, but soon this too came to an end.

Time after time, too numerous to count, Father Drolet has made his voice heard, and time after time he has been transferred. I often think what good bishops these young priests would make. Being transferred all over the diocese, they get to know it as few others can.

I can see Father Drolet, rising up from his breakfast table, after Mass, after reading the daily paper, and going along that ugly highway to the beautiful city of New Orleans and passing through those streets of such beautiful names—Elysian Fields, Gentilly, Justice, Piety, Plenty, Benefit, Agriculture, Pleasure, Humanity, Desire. I see him standing there beside that intrepid Methodist minister whose house and church have been defiled, whose wife and children have been threatened, whose phone rings with obscenity in the dead of the night. And I am proud of this Methodist minister and this Catholic priest.

The opposition to integration, led by Catholics, sad to say, filled the Civic auditorium. The White Citizens Council takes the place now of the Ku Klux Klan. "It reminds you of the early days of Nazism," Father Drolet said. "They have a well-organized public relations department which provides material for press and radio. And people are afraid, afraid for their jobs. The press reported that it was the parents of the children going to the two schools where they were beginning token integration who were making the protest, making up the mob, but one should not believe them! They were not young parents but a group of much older women from other parts of town, manipulated to make a mob. Everyone is afraid and the police do not stop them."

"There is fear of course of physical violence," Father Drolet went on, "but mostly it is fear of losing jobs. And those people up North who read about these things should look to themselves too," he said, smiling. "We read down here about New Rochelle and Levittown, and Chicago, the housing projects, the discrimination practiced there in housing, jobs and schools."

Had he suffered from telephone calls and violence, we asked Father Drolet. No, but the White Citizens Council circulated leaflets outside of his church after every Mass on Sunday, stating that he was being investigated by the House Un-American Activities Committee. He and his custodian and his parishioners had tried to collect the leaflets from the windshields of the cars around. The custodian had been arrested. That's the heartbreaking thing about it, that it is the Negroes who are made to suffer, just as in South Africa when the priests and ministers open the churches to them and beg them to come in.

I was told by another priest who had seen the leaflet that Father Drolet was accused of circulating the *Daily Worker* when he was in the seminary. It was *The Catholic Worker* they were referring to, perhaps.

~

Here in Baton Rouge I am staying in a colored parish, with members of Caritas, which is a new secular institute in formation, made up of Negroes and whites. We had been with the Caritas branch in New Orleans and had seen some bad slums—unpaved streets, sewerless neighborhoods, and sinking houses in the inadequately filled-in land of the town dump and the swamps. Now we were in the outskirts of Baton Rouge, in a more picturesque section, where the church, St. Paul's, is just around a bend in the road, and is a rebuilt movie house. The parish hall is a rebuilt saloon and it is there I am going to speak this "evening," as they say, though it will be only two p.m.

Father Osborne, the pastor here, has long been a friend, whom I first met at Collegeville, in Minnesota. When I arrived at the hall, there were some of his former parishioners from the little parish across the river where he had been for seven years. He has been only seven months in this parish but has already accomplished wonders.

Father Osborne is a large man of great dignity, especially in his magnificent vestments, hand-woven of raw silk, made in Switzerland and in Prinknash Abbey in Gloucester, England. Over the altar of his church there is a great crucifix, painted by Dom Gregory de Witte, a Swiss artist, who painted the colorful refectory at St. Joseph's Abbey at Covington, Louisiana. There are paintings of St. Paul on one side and Our Lady on the other.

There was a baptism here this morning before the six-thirty Mass, and the tall, young colored man wore a white garment rather like a chasuble, but simpler since it was two pieces of white linen cloth, hanging down front and back and joined at the shoulders by tapes tied. There have been seventy-four baptisms these last seven months. Converts have come from Southern University (colored), as well as from the neighborhood.

One might say that Father Osborne's parish is the first integrated parish under a Negro pastor. Perhaps his white parishioners from his former parish, where the white priest Father James Clement was his former pastor, led the way. The parish covers three little towns, Rosedale, Marin Gouin ("big mosquito") and Grosse Tete ("big head").

One of the teachers at the Shady Grove High School here was staying at Caritas with us this weekend, and she told me about a small group of the teachers at her school. When the trouble started, they recognized the danger of violence and loss of job, but they resolved on a course of action. They sent a telegram, also signed by twenty-five others, to the Legislature, which is made up mostly of northern and rural people who are against integration, and said firmly that they upheld the ruling of the Supreme Court.

Since then there have been community meetings discussing this, the latest a week ago. A town committee has been set up within the community to investigate the teachers, and smear tactics have been used. The additional twenty-five signers have been brainwashed, the committee says, but threats are made against them too. The community involved numbers only about two thousand people, which makes it all the more courageous for the thirty-one involved to take the stand they did.

Another outstanding figure in the struggle is Doug Manship, who owns the Baton Rouge broadcasting company and the television station. He reaches the public on the side of the few courageous ones with editorials which come out weekly.

One must not forget to mention Rudolph Lombard, student at Xavier University of New Orleans, which is run by the Sisters of the Blessed Sacrament. He was arrested in the sit-ins, and is now under sentence of sixty days and two hundred and fifty dollar fine, which is being appealed. He is a member of CORE, the Committee for Racial Equality. He is a tall young Negro, a good student and well-liked by his companions. There are also the demonstrations of the thousands of Southern University students who marched on the State Capitol at Baton Rouge, and the eighteen who were arrested there.

~

I felt when I left New Orleans that I had scarcely scratched the surface in finding out what was going on. Then, picking up the paper this morning, I read of fighting in Rwanda and Angola, in Laos and in Ecuador, where herdsmen and agricultural workers are battling the landowners with spears and war drums. Scattered and sporadic, these revolts are part of a world movement among the poor and despised.

Here in America, these educated students are using the weapons of nonviolence against discrimination, and we who are writing and reporting must tell of these things to give courage to other isolated groups who feel alone and ineffectual.

The National Catholic Conference for Interracial Justice concluded a two-day meeting in Washington, D.C., with this statement, referring to the 1960 Bishops' statement on personal responsibility. "There comes a time, and this is one in Louisiana, when private attitude and action is an insufficient display of just attitudes and of a willingness to do right . . . give open support to constructive steps forward, otherwise the racist will lead; and if such is the case, the right thinking but silent man shares the responsibility for this evil."

Father Jerome Drolet has done this. Father Osborne has done this, and so have these teachers and students I have written about. They have risked physical violence and loss of job. I have met with these people and without doubt there are more we don't read about in the press.

"Perhaps," said Father Drolet, the "South will lead yet, in this struggle, in spite of everything."

Certainly, and best of all, it is the Negroes who have furnished the inspired leadership of the countless thousands in the Montgomery bus strike and in the sit-in strikes which are still going on all over the South. The imprisonments of so many, the buffetings, the being spat upon, burned with cigarette butts, the ordeal of facing even with their little children the screaming hatred of mobs—all this gives so great a demonstration of nonviolence that it blinds us, perhaps, to the importance of what is going on. These are the weapons of the spirit, these sufferings.

# 'A. J.'                                                    36

---

Death of a peacemaker.

---

ABRAHAM JOHANNES MUSTE of the War Resisters League,
known to millions as A. J., died on February 11th at three o'clock
in the afternoon at St. Luke's Hospital, in New York. He had not been ill
a day. That morning he had woken up suffering pains in the back, and
his doctor had urged him to go to St. Luke's. Soon after he entered the
hospital he lapsed into unconsciousness and died most peacefully. His
had been a long and a happy life of work for brotherhood and peace.

Muste had given us the story of his early life in an uncompleted
autobiography which is included in a volume called *The Essays of A. J.
Muste,* edited by Nat Hentoff and published by Bobbs-Merrill. He was
born in a small Dutch town of so little importance that its name was
treated with derision, as Bohunk is here, or Wigan Pier is in England.
"Can anything good come out of Nazareth?" comes to mind. His father
was a coachman for a rich family who lived in what seemed to him a
palace. His own family lived in one room, with alcoves for beds. He remembers having the job of fetching the morning porridge from a community kitchen for the employer's big family, and how heavy the kettle
was in the cold and dark of early morning. He was five or six then. He
doesn't mention being hungry ever, so perhaps his mother, who was
gay and smiling (she played the part of Santa Claus at Christmas time)
fed him before he set out.

Originally published in *Commonweal,* March 24, 1967. Vol. LXXXVI, 14–16.

When on the insistence of his mother's brothers, and with the offer of a loan for passage in steerage, the whole family spent two weeks at sea in midwinter with their own provisions, and the mother became ill and had to be hospitalized, the father easily substituted for her, and there is no mention of hardship because of the mother's absence. Indeed, the father took the children to a window on deck where they could greet their mother and see her smiling face. Because of her illness, they had to stay on Ellis Island for a month, and they used to play through the halls, with never a rebuke, because they were well-behaved children. Indeed, one senses that the Dutch were welcome guests in this new land, diligent and Protestant as they were.

One always thinks of the Calvinists as a dour people, but Muste's reminiscences are happy ones. At the first sound of the church bells on Sunday, a "jubilant" announcement, he calls it, the way to church and the time in church "are a delight, and the entrance into it, an entering into another world, the real world, the feeling which later I found conveyed in one of the New Testament Epistles, that one had come to the city of the living God."

He did not despise the "little way," the small incident. He tells of only one, and there must have been many, but he was not setting out to write a spiritual autobiography. The story he tells is of the mischievous boy he was, putting out his foot and tripping up a bully, older and larger than he, who had been called up for reprimand to the teacher's desk. The stumbling was taken as further horseplay and the boy was reprimanded twice over. The rest of the day the young A. J. knew that there would be an encounter when they got out of sight of the school, and he does not say that he was not afraid. When the meeting took place and the other boy's opening words were, "You tripped me," he looked his adversary in the eye and admitted it. Strangely enough, the larger boy turned on his heel and the anticipated retribution did not take place. Muste saw this incident as important; he had learned to face up to an adversary, look him in the eye, to admit the truth and not try to justify himself, and, most important of all, to overcome fear. I am sure that the "gentleness" that Père Régamey extols was present in his eye and speech, as it always was, and no hint of making judgment of a *person*, only of a way of acting.

That is one of the things I always felt about A. J., and one of the reasons the young trusted him and listened to him. There was little question of age difference. They were on the same side, and they trusted him in spite of his age. There was no malice in him, and so he found no malice in others. I am not saying that he did not make moral judgments. His whole life was testimony to that. On the one side was life, and on the other death, and he chose life. He kept the commandments, and Jesus promised, to those who loved God and their brother, "Do this and thou shalt live."

The first school A. J. went to back in Grand Rapids, Michigan, was a religious school, and in first grade he was put to memorizing the 119th Psalm (which happens to be my own favorite). His sister started school when he was ready for second grade, and from then on all the children of the Muste family went to public schools. They could not afford the religious school run by the Dutch Reformed Church. After all, his father had begun his work in this country at six dollars for a sixty-hour week.

A. J. tells us little of his private life. He mentions that when he graduated from the seminary in Holland, Michigan, he spent a year in the ministry in a small town in Iowa, where he met the young woman who was to be his wife. He fell in love at first sight, married young and had a happy married life for the next forty-five years. He got degrees from New Brunswick Theological Seminary and from Union Theological Seminary in New York, and served in New York churches, one of them on Second Avenue and Seventh Street. He became acquainted with the narrow streets of the lower East Side, with the poor of every nationality clustered there.

He gave up his first fulltime assignment to a church in the suburbs of Boston when the United States entered the First World War, began working in Providence with Quakers, and was accepted by them in their ministry some time later. (It was as a Quaker minister that he married my only sister's only daughter, Sue Spier, to Mikio Miyake, a young Japanese scientist, born in Hiroshima and now working at the University of Washington.)

### The Textile Strikes

Loving Emerson as he did, and following in Thoreau's footsteps in his espousal of civil disobedience (he called it "holy disobedience"), he enjoyed living in New England. Together with a number of other clergymen he participated in 1919 in the second big Lawrence, Massachusetts, textile strike, and took a leading part. It was only the first of many labor situations he became involved in, an involvement so deep that it took him for a time into the Trotskyist movement and led to a visit with Trotsky in Norway, at the invitation of that exponent of perpetual revolution. As secretary of the Amalgamated Textile Workers of America, Muste participated and led many strikes in the textile field and gained a thorough knowledge of the labor movement.

Peter Maurin was the first one of our Catholic Worker family to meet A. J. He had heard of him in Union Square as a Trotskyite, and when A. J. became head of the Presbyterian Labor Temple on Second Avenue and Fourteenth Street, he sought him out there for discussion. Peter talked at length and with animation, and I can see A. J., who respected all men, listening carefully, because Peter's accent was hard to get used to, and he was accustomed to talking until he felt he had made his point. Then he would wait for the other man to make his. Peter's idea of a good conversation was one between two people, with other listeners to the dialogue, provided they did not butt in. Such a conversation could go on for a long time, because A. J. knew how to listen, and since he listened with respect for the one who was speaking to him, he made others respect that other also, and try to understand his point of view.

Peter had read us Berdyaev's *Christianity and Class War,* and it was Muste's essay, "Pacifism and Class War," which had first interested him in Muste. The essays, "Trade Unions and the Revolution" and "Return to Pacifism," written in 1935 and 1936, clearly show what attracted Peter to Muste's meetings. Reading Muste's essays, as I am doing now, I am refreshed and stimulated and happy indeed that there is this record left of the life of a great and good man whose influence will long be felt. It is a great heavy book and weighs a ton, and I'm hoping that it will soon be in paperback so that we will see young people reading it on picket lines, sit-ins and in courts while they await sentencing for the witness they are giving to their faith in the ideas that A. J. set forth so brilliantly for so long.

Years ago, when we were having a conference of peace leaders at the Catholic Worker Farm in Newburgh one winter, one quality in A. J. struck me forcibly, and that is that there was no aggression in his speech or demeanor. While the Catholics felt called upon to express themselves vehemently, one might almost say aggressively, A. J. kept a peaceful calm that could not help but permeate the rather hectic atmosphere. There was a quality of silence about him that everyone remarked at the meetings which were held after his death, and he was not impatient to be heard, or to get his word in. He enjoyed listening to others, one felt, and was not just waiting to have his say, to be heard. And he had plenty to say. He could sum things up succinctly enough at a small gathering, but when he was invited to speak at a meeting he spoke at length, with no gesturing, no "eloquence." You listened to what he had to say, not to how he said it.

But the last time I "heard" him speak, I did not hear him speak, because I was behind the platform set up at Union Square, and the microphones carried his voice across the square even to the opposition that was picketing on the other side. The two of us were there, both of us speaking, to uphold the young men who were about to burn their draft cards in order to dramatize most seriously their opposition to the war in Vietnam, and to conscription, which forced eighteen-year-olds into an army which was committing such atrocities against women and children with their napalm and lazy dog bombs, a war in which every condition for a just war was being violated. There was a terrible threat of violence that day in the air, in the crowd before us as well as in the pickets in the distance. And that there was hostility in this crowd was shown by the man who had a fire extinguisher under his coat and turned it on the draft-card burners. Cries rang out—"Why not acid instead of water?" The water was sprayed over A. J. and me too, and it put out the flames of the draft cards but he stood there calmly as the counter-demonstrators shouted, "Burn yourselves, not your draft cards!" A. J. had spoken about the death of Norman Morrison, the Quaker who had immolated himself in front of the Pentagon not long before, and of Alice Herz, the Jewish refugee who was the first person in the United States to offer her life in a flaming protest against what men of her adopted country were doing to each other at the other end of the world. It was two or three days after that noon rally in Union Square that Roger LaPorte set fire to himself in front of the United Nations.

~

I cannot close this little obituary without quoting a few lines from a book I am reading now. *The Two-Edged Sword*, by Father John L. McKenzie, S.J., written back in 1955, an interpretation of the Old Testament. Father McKenzie writes, "We must not underestimate the creative powers of the human genius. . . . What makes the history of the human race differ from the history of the anthropoid ape is the rare but recurring emergence of men who can break out of the framework of their times and initiate a new departure." I could not help but think of A. J. Muste and how in a new era of violence, he has epitomized the concept of nonviolence, in correlating the material and the spiritual, in this secular age.

# Dorothy Day on Hope $37$

Q. Are you in general optimistic or pessimistic about the future of reform in the church?

A. The kind of controversy going on in the church today is certainly resulting in "clarification of thought," to use a cliché which Peter Maurin, founder of the Catholic Worker, did not hesitate to use as emphasizing the necessity for this clear thinking to precede any program of action. "Wisdom is more active than all active things," *Wisdom 7:24*. Authority and freedom, man and the state, war and peace on the home front as well as abroad, these are the great issues today and include the problems of poverty, population explosion and race relations. My concern is that the controversies be carried on without violence. To me, nonviolence is the all important problem or virtue, to be nourished and cultivated. "Language can as validly be used to repel thrusts or to assert dominance as can fists and guns," Stan Windass writes in a recent *PAX* bulletin from England. "Judge not that ye be not judged," is the title of the excerpt and it is part of his pamphlet or booklet, *A Blow for Peace*, one of a *Where We Stand* series, published by Darton, Longmans and Todd in England. The ideas in this have dominated my thinking for the past six months. One has to begin by doing violence to

Originally published in *Commonweal*, November 14, 1969. Vol. XCI, 217–18.

one's self to grow in love and understanding of our enemies, and sometimes the worst of these enemies have been of our own household, as Jesus said they would. I'm thinking of the Vietnam War and the bishops, but it applies daily to those close to you in work or parish or community. But "the anger of man worketh not the righteousness of God," St. James wrote two thousand years ago. It certainly helps in keeping the joyous spirit which comes with love. How can I have anything else but hope and confidence, reading the prophets on these ember days, those prophets which Father John McKenzie has helped me to understand? "Do not be sad, for the joy of the Lord is our strength."

Let me thank *Commonweal* for printing those occasional papers, *God, Jesus* and *Holy Spirit*. They formed the basis for our third Sunday discussions at the Catholic Worker farm last winter. I like to recall St. Teresa's remark, "I am so grateful a creature that I can be bought with a sardine." (I've lost track of where I've read it.) And certainly we at the Catholic Worker are grateful too. *Commonweal's* George Shuster sent Peter Maurin to me in 1932, and Ed Skillin and countless others on the staff have supported us in many ways and with all kinds of help, nourishing and warming us mentally and physically. So I'm glad to have the opportunity to say thank you.

And oh yes, why worry about empty schools, seminars and even rectories? Maybe the Lord is giving us a little reminder that there has been too much building going on, and that it is time to use some of these buildings for the poor, for families. Out in Milwaukee evicted families were moving into empty army barracks. I've heard of Sacred Heart nuns using an empty novitiate for a daycare center for the children of the poor, and Redemptorist sisters making room for aged senile patients put out of a mental hospital during a recent strike. The State interferes, of course, but perhaps it is time the sisters were taught holy disobedience as a loving and nonviolent way to combat bureaucracy.

The problem of the Papal States was cleared up over the last 100 years (after a fashion), and certainly the financial problems of too much money and too many investments will also be taken care of, one way or another. "This corruption must put on incorruption," as St. Paul wrote, and while the outer body is falling apart, the inner is being renewed! Shocking and stimulating thoughts for us all.

# A Reminiscence at 75          38

Dorothy Day, cofounder of the Catholic Worker movement, wrote her first article for *Commonweal* in September of 1929. To mark her 75th birthday, the editors recently asked her for an article of reminiscence and recollection. Her response follows.

D EAR FRIENDS,

I hope you do not mind my responding to your request for a short "reminiscence" by writing you a rather disjointed letter. I am inspired today by a great sense of happiness and gratitude to God and to *Commonweal* too and a desire to share it. I wonder how many people realize the loneliness of the convert. I don't know whether I conveyed that in my book *The Long Loneliness.* I wrote in my book about giving up a lover. But it meant also giving up a whole society of friends and fellow workers. It was such a betrayal of them, they thought. One who had yearned to walk in the footsteps of a Mother Jones and an Emma Goldman seemingly had turned her back on the entire radical movement and sought shelter in that great, corrupt Holy Roman Catholic Church, right hand of the Oppressor, the State, rich and heartless, a traitor to her beginnings, her Founder, etc.

Originally published in *Commonweal*, August 10, 1973. Vol. XCV, 424–5.

Anatole France introduced me to the Desert Fathers in his book *Thais,* and even in that satire the beauty of the saints shone through. George Eliot introduced me to the mystics. Her Maggie Tulliver read the *Imitation,* so I read it too, regardless of the fact that George Eliot rejected formal religion. Did you know that Tolstoy has Pierre read the *Imitation* after his duel with his wife's lover? That Gandhi and Vinoba Bhave have read the *Imitation?* And Pope John? It still nourishes me. I'm tired of hearing eminent theologians disparagingly quote that line, "I never go out into the company of men without coming back less a man." But how much idle talk in all our lives, dishonesty, equivocation, and so forth sullying each precious day! I go down on my knees each night and say "Dear Father, Jesus told us you were Our Father, repair these slips, mistakes, even sins I have committed with my tongue during this day—the discouraging word, the biting criticism, etc." Even this article.

Of course "my bitterness was most bitter" over and over again, not at Holy Mother the Church but at the human element in it. But thank God, there were always the Saints. When I visited Cuba and recalled Fr. Las Casas and all he was reputed to have done for the Indians, a Communist friend said grimly, "Yes, but as a landowner which he originally was, he introduced African slavery because the Indians died under the hard work, and besides he liked them better than the Africans."

I looked at the biography of Las Casas in the *Catholic Encyclopedia* and found that there was quite a bit of truth in that.

God forgive us the sins of our youth! But as Zachariah sang out, "We have knowledge of salvation through *forgiveness of our sins.*" I don't think anyone recognizes the comfort of this text better than I do. I have not yet been attracted by the present tendency to bring everything out into the light of day by public and published confessions. Were we not taught by Holy Mother Church to respect the modesty of the confessional? Or is that a silly expression? But oh the joy of knowing that you can always go there and be forgiven seventy times seven times. (Even though you wonder, in your distrust of yourself, whether you *really* mean or have the strength to "amend your life.") I hope your readers can read between the lines from the above and recognize what my positions on birth control and abortion are.

When I visited Australia (where there is a CW paper, a house of hospitality and a farming commune of families) newspaper reporters on my arrival in Melbourne and Sydney asked me what was my position on the Berrigans, birth control and abortion. My answer was simplistic.

I followed Pope Paul. As to the Berrigans, I did not know what the Pope's attitude was, but I was a follower of Gandhi and Vinoba Bhave and in spite of the Berrigans' innocently destructive tendencies, loved them both.

Thank God we have a Pope Paul who upholds *respect for life*, an ideal so lofty, so high, so important even when it seems he has the whole Catholic world against him. Peter Maurin always held before our eyes a vision of the new man, the new social order as being possible, by God's grace, here and now, and he so fully lived the life of voluntary poverty and manual labor and he spent so much time in silence, and an hour a day in church, besides daily Mass and Communion (while he was in the city), that all who knew him revered and loved him as the leader and inspirer of the Catholic Worker movement. As for me, I am so much a woman, that I am the housekeeper of the CW movement. And I am a journalist and well trained in that, what with a father and three brothers, all of whom were journalists.

To get down to my gratitude to *Commonweal* which helped to train me in my journalistic career. George Shuster, of *Commonweal* in 1932, sent Peter Maurin to me. Not only that, whenever the CW appealed for help the *Commonweal* staff (I could not name all that contributed to us), not only sent money and clothes. They even shared their yearly retreats which they used to make at Portsmouth Priory when they invited some of our crowd, editor or a Bowery resident.

Peter Maurin used to bring some of our brilliant young men, like John Cogley, to visit the editors of *Commonweal*. He told me that John should be an editor of *Commonweal* some day. Peter thought of the CW as a school always and when he started having nightly meetings those first years, *Commonweal* helped provide speakers, besides building up our prestige so that we got many famous men over the years. Space forbids listing them.

Peter was delighted when people praised him and even seemed to boast of the college presidents who listened to him. He thought prestige helped the work. "We need to build up the prestige of these young men," he said to me and he himself did it to such an extent that many a time he was foolhardy in his trust and estimate of others.

I must illustrate my own explanation of why I have accepted the awards that have been accorded to me in the past few years, by a little story. This is called "reminiscing" and serves to remind people that I am *very, very old*, as one of my grandchildren said to me once. She said it as she handed me a crude drawing of a ten-tiered, high-riser birthday cake, "because you are *very, very old*," she had printed underneath, and have nine grandchildren to eat that cake, she neglected to add.

The story is this. A girl called Katey Smith way back in '34 was sent us by St. Vincent's Hospital; she had been operated on for tumor of the brain. (She recovered.) She loved to join in all our activities and accompanied us on a picketing expedition one day on 34th Street in front of the Mexican Consulate because renewed persecution of the Church had broken out. A passerby asked her what the picket line was about and she answered, "None of your damn business."

I would feel like Katey Smith if I refused some of the honors offered me, honors which call attention to and pay tribute to Peter Maurin's ideas. I have refused honorary degrees because of my respect for Holy Wisdom, just as much as for my abhorrence of our military-industrial-agricultural-educational-complex-conglomerate. I compromised when I accepted the Laetare medal from Notre Dame this year. Fr. Hesburgh threatened to come to First Street and present it there if I did not come to the midwest. At the Notre Dame graduation and conferral of degrees, a dozen or so honorary ones, I could be lost in the crowd, I thought. So I accepted and could acknowledge my debts of gratitude to George Shuster, who is assistant to the president, and Julian Pleasants and Norrie Merdzinsky who with various Holy Cross Fathers and Brothers and students kept a house of hospitality going in South Bend for some years. The Pleasants, the Ryans, the Geisslers, the McKiernans and others kept the idea of communal rural living, and intellectual work and manual labor alive all these years; and William Storey, a professor at Notre Dame who has fed my spiritual life for many years by his set of books—*Days of the Lord,* excerpts from which gave me the energy this morning to sit down and write this very imperfect letter of thanks to my friends.

I write this from my place of semi-retirement at Tivoli, New York. The spirit of youth today rejects our old names, *Maryfarm* and *St. Joseph's House,* but still keeps the name "Catholic Worker Farm." It is not the kind of farming commune or agronomic university Peter Maurin envisaged, but we can boast that whereas the average age of most "communes" in the U.S. today, according to statistics (Stanley Vishnewski says), is nine months (if you know better, write to him), our own commune has lasted thirty-eight years. The first farm was started in 1934, and there are still old-timers here, John Filliger, Hans Tunnesen, Stanley Vishnewski, Marge Hughes, Slim, etc. The latter three arriving when they were seventeen. Fidelity, constancy, are beautiful words, but we must confess there is much plain stubbornness and very real poverty, even destitution, which holds us together too.

Thank you for your patience. If you don't want this letter-article, send it back and I will use or expand on it for my next "On Pilgrimage" column in the *CW*. Fr. Clarence Duffy who was with us during the war years used to do the like. If we cut paragraphs from one of his articles, he used to gather them together from the wastepaper basket and paste them into his next article.

Love and gratitude to all of you always.

# Index

abortion, 129, 166
Amalgamated Textile Workers of
    America, 161
*America*, xiii
anarchism, 104
Association of Catholic Trade
    Unionists, 61
Auden, W. H., xiii, 136
Austen, Jane, 137

Baird, Peggy, 85–6
Baton Rouge, 153, 155–6
Beck, Judith, 134–8
Berdyaev, Nicholai, 161
Bernanos, Georges, xiii, 110
Berrigan, Daniel, xiii, 166–7
Berrigan, Philip, xiii, 166–7
Bethune, Ade, 61, 74, 106
Bhave, Vinoba, 166–7
birth control, 166–7
Boston, 57–8, 62, 147–8, 160
bus trips, 111–16, 145–6

Callahan, William, 61, 74
Capri, 26, 99
Caritas, 155–6
Casey, Marion, 151
Catholic University, 67, 122

Catholic Worker movement, xi–xiv,
    57–66, 74, 76, 80–3, 85–6, 89,
    104–11, 121–3, 132, 142, 146–7, 150,
    155, 163–9
Chesterton, G. K., xiii, 45
civil defense drills, 133
civil disobedience, 120, 130, 133, 160,
    162
Cogley, John, xiii, 110, 167
Columbia University, 122
*Commonweal*, xi–xiv, 74, 76, 102, 105,
    107, 110, 117, 119, 139, 164–5, 167
Communists, 40, 60, 85–6, 88, 105,
    123, 143, 166
CORE, 156
Cort, John, 61, 123, 132

Dawson, Christopher, 117
Day, Dorothy, xi–xiv, 102
Day, John, 25, 35, 54
Debs, Eugene, 77
De las Casas, Bartolome, 14, 166
Dempsey, Jack, 85
de Witte, Grergory, 155
Dickens, Charles, 26, 50, 113
Diego, Juan, 8, 10, 144
Dostoevsky, Fyodor, 137
Doukhobors, 137